FINAL TOU

Stories of Devon Aircrew
and
RAF Bases in South and East Devon

Researched by
Grahame Holloway
for
The East Devon Branch of The AirCrew Association.

**The aircraft on the front cover is a Hurricane of
No.504 Squadron based at Exeter in 1940 whilst that
above is of a Mosquito operated by CAACU at Exeter
in the 1950's.**

Published by:

' BREVET 2000 '

**The Publishing Section
of the
East Devon Branch of The AirCrew Association.
The RAFA Club
Imperial Road, Exmouth.**

**Printed by:
SPEED PRINT
Unit 29, Dinan Way Trading Estate,
Concorde Road
Exmouth, EX8 4RS**

First Published 2005

ISBN 0-9539015-2-1

2

Contents

Dedication and Acknowledgements   4

Introduction   5

About the Author   6

The AirCrew Association   7

The Story behind a Gavel   9

Introduction to airfields   11

RAF Poltimore   12

RAF Exminster   15

RAF Exeter   17

RAF Dunkeswell   22

RAF Upottery   25

RNAS Haldon   30

RAF Bolt Head   35

RAF Roborough   37

RAF Harrowbeer   39

RAF Okehampton (Folly Gate)   42

RAF Mount Batten   45

RAF Marine Branch   49

The Role of Local Hotels   57

The Plymouth Hoe AirCrew Memorial   79

Introduction to Members' Service Histories   81

The personal aviation histories of local aircrew   82

Photographs of other featured aircraft   213

Glossary and RAF ranks   218

With thanks to our Sponsors   219

DEDICATION

This book is dedicated to all aircrew,
whether still flying or having made their
'Final Touchdown', who have served in the armed forces of
Her Majesty or Her Allies and have been awarded an
approved brevet recognising their training to operate as a
skilled member of the aircrew fraternity.

ACKNOWLEDGEMENT

Grateful thanks go to all those members of the East Devon, Torbay and Plymouth Branches of The AirCrew Association who, reluctantly in some cases, have provided the material to make this book possible. Also acknowledged is the great help given by Dick Ward and Tim Liles in undertaking the proof reading and the many others who, behind the scenes, provided photographs and encouragement.

However we also owe a great debt of gratitude to *'Awards for All'* whose generous grant, together with sponsorship donations from others mentioned later, have made this publication possible. Without their support the stories related within these pages would have remained forever untold.

All profits arising from the sale of this book will be distributed by the Committee of the East Devon Branch of The AirCrew Association in furtherance of the Association's aims and such charities as may be supported by it.

INTRODUCTION

"Final Touchdown" is the third book to be published by the East Devon Branch of The AirCrew Association, the first being *"Touchdown - East Devon" (1997)* and *"East Devon Aircrew & Airfields" (2000)*.   Together they featured the service careers of over ninety members of the Branch ranging from the stalwarts of World War II, lowly National Service pilots of the 1950's to those who served through the more recent conflicts of the Falklands and the Gulf. All have had interesting tales to tell.

As the years pass those heroes of World War II are now in their 80's and sadly over a quarter of those whose stories were told in our first book have since taken up permanent residence in the sky.   We still miss them but have some comfort in the thought that at least their stories will remain to be read by those who follow.   In compiling *'Final Touchdown'* we record further stories of those who have served their country in the air. However, in addition to members of the East Devon Branch, we have now cast the net further to include our colleagues in the Torbay and Plymouth Branches of The AirCrew Association and their contributions have been gratefully received.

The war-time role of the RAF Stations of East Devon was covered in some detail in the first two books so in this edition we also look at those situated in the South of the County, viz. Haldon, Bolt Head, Roborough, Harrowbeer and Folly Gate, together with the maritime base at Mount Batten and the dangerous work of the RAF's Air-Sea Rescue Service in saving airmen who 'ditched in the drink'.   Finally, the role played by many of Torbay's hotels in providing the initial training for young aircrew recruits and hospital facilities for injured aircrew is acknowledged.

The Author

As you will discover, this work contains recollections and reminiscences from many sources. These have been researched by **Grahame Holloway** to provide the third in a trilogy of books recounting the service life of local aircrew, and facts behind some of our wartime air bases.

A former RAF National Service pilot, Grahame trained in Canada on T-6's in the early 1950's. Returning to the UK, he converted onto the de Havilland Vampire before seeing further service with the RAFVR and R.Aux.AF. Later, during the height of the *'Cold War'* and whilst pursuing a career in the Police Service, he was one of only a handful of police officers trained for specialist flying duties should a nuclear attack be made on Britain. He retired in 1986 as a Superintendent.

Post retirement, he served with the Royal Observer Corps until its disbandment in September 1991. As a Group Officer his RAF connections occasionally saw him flying on sorties with Nimrods of No. 42 Squadron, RAF St. Mawgan, and on Hercules training flights from RAF Lyneham. A former Chairman, he is currently Hon. Secretary of the East Devon Branch of the AirCrew Association. His hobbies include travel and writing. As well as the author of the two previous books in this series, his other works include *"Copper's Devon"* and *"Battles, Bullets & Mayhem"*.

The AirCrew Association.

The bond between those who have flown and known the comradeship of Service life is a strong one, further strengthened by the fact that their environment was the sky, majestic and without boundaries yet concealing many dangers. Threats from the enemy faced many, for others their fight was against the elements. It is not surprising, therefore, that this special bond resulted in the formation of The AirCrew Association whose membership is uniquely limited to those who have served as aircrew in the armed forces of Her Majesty, or Her Allies, and have been awarded a 'recognised flying badge'. Today it comprises not only pilots and navigators but the veteran air gunners, bomb aimers, flight engineers and wireless operators of WWII together with the air electronics and weapon systems operators, helicopter winchmen and air loadmasters of the modern age.

There are around a hundred branches in Britain of which four will be found in the southern half of Devon, namely the East Devon, Torbay, Kingsbridge and Plymouth branches. Overseas, they exist from Australia and New Zealand to South Africa, the United States and Canada, all linked by the Association's quarterly Magazine, *'Intercom'*. *'The AirCrew Association Charitable Fund'*, registered as a charity, exists to provide speedy 'FIRST AID' to members in need whilst, additionally, the *'AirCrew Association Archive Trust'* recognises the importance of preserving aircrew archives and memorabilia for future generations to study and enjoy. The Trust's aim is to preserve such items and it now has a permanent home and display at the Yorkshire Air Museum.

The East Devon Branch was founded by Don Francis, a former navigator who flew Mosquitoes with a 'special duties' squadron during the war and later became the Chief Draughtsman for the De Havilland Blue Streak project. It began life as the Exmouth & District Branch in February 1991 but since then it has grown into one of the most active in the country and had to change its name to 'East Devon' to more accurately describe the area from which its current membership of over ninety is drawn. Meetings are held at the RAFA Club, Imperial Road, Exmouth, at 7.30 pm on the 2nd Tuesday of each month. These are complemented by a full social programme which includes pub lunches, buffets, dinner-dances and visits to interesting venues and events. An informative monthly newsletter also keeps members 'in touch' on a number of issues.

East Devon Branch Founder, Don Francis and a welcoming corner of
Exmouth RAFA Club.

Next in size, with over forty members, is the Torbay Branch which holds its monthly meetings at The Paignton Club, situated at the harbour end of the town's Esplanade. These are morning meetings held on the 3rd Tuesday at 1030 am. Members of the other two branches mentioned also meet regularly and all are pleased to welcome new members .

The Story behind the Gavel !

At first sight, just an ordinary gavel !   In fact this one is used by the Chairman of the East Devon Branch of The AirCrew Association on the occasion of the business element of their meetings.   Presented by their President, Joe Williams, in December 1995 it has a unique history which is worthy of recounting here.

A Sergeant Air Gunner, who occupied the tail turret of a Lancaster bomber, Joe Williams' flying career with No. 625 Squadron came to an abrupt end on March 5th 1945 whilst engaged on a raid on Chemnitz, deep into Eastern Germany and close to the Czech border.   The omens were not good from the start for their aircraft, known on the squadron as 'Fox Two' and with Serial Number NG240, suffered an engine loss before they had even cleared the English coast on the outward leg. An impromptu vote amongst the crew decided they should 'press on regardless'. Unfortunately, one engine short and with a full bomb load, they could not keep up with the main bomber stream and although they reached their target it was not before the others were on their way home.

Alone and in a hostile environment, they were attacked by a German night-fighter and, although the bomber crew put up a brave defence, the Lancaster was seriously damaged by the enemy's cannon fire and burst into flames. Joe and his colleagues were forced to bale out of their burning aircraft and landed relatively safely over the Czech border. Although subsequently taken prisoner Joe eventually escaped whilst on a forced-march and remained free until reaching the advancing US Forces.

He often wondered what happened to his aircraft and in 1987 he learned from Czech friends that its wreckage had been discovered in a forest. Furthermore, his rear turret had been located and taken to the National Aviation Museum in Prague. Elated by this news, the following year Joe returned to Czechoslovakia and was taken to the crash site where some pieces of wreckage still remained. Amongst the few fragments he collected as souvenirs was a brass return valve from one of the aircraft's Merlin engines. It was this which he later incorporated into the gavel which he fashioned from the wood of an oak tree in the garden of his Exton home.

The decision of the crew to 'Press on Regardless' was later captured by the Australian aviation artist John Castle in a painting of the same name and shows Joe's aircraft, with one engine feathered, crossing the coast at Beachy Head. In 2005 Joe and Cliff Lear, the Flight Engineer on that fateful flight, were guests of the Czech Authorities at their celebrations commemorating the 60th anniversary of the end of WWII. Sadly, Cliff died from a heart attack in his Prague hotel.

The Royal Air Force

in

East and South Devon

The Westland Lysander was used for a number of tasks including Army Co-operation. Its short landing and take-off capability also made it an ideal aircraft for deployment of agents in and out of occupied France. A versatile aircraft, No. 276 Squadron operated them from RAF Harrowbeer in an Air Sea Rescue role during 1942 but they also made frequent flights from many other Devon airfields.

The Royal Air Force in East and South Devon

As stated in the introduction, the role of the RAF in East Devon during WWII and immediately afterwards, has been covered in some depth in the first two books of this series.   However, for those who have not had the opportunity of reading them an abridged account is included here. In addition the geographical boundaries have been stretched to include other RAF bases which were located in the southern half of the county. Neither has the vital and often dangerous role of the RAF's marine branch with their high-speed air-sea rescue launches been overlooked, nor the vital part played by many of the county's hotels.   Many former aircrew, now living locally, have added their reminiscences and in some instances a brief synopsis of their service history has been included. In such cases their full stories have already been included in the earlier editions, either in *'Touchdown East Devon'* or *'East Devon Aircrew and Airfields'*.

It is an inescapable fact that no RAF operation in the air would be successful without the co-ordination of the ground based controllers. It is therefore perhaps fitting to start with the role of RAF 10 Group Sector Control at RAF Poltimore.

RAF POLTIMORE

This site, now largely derelict, lies in the parkland of 16th century Poltimore House on the eastern outskirts of Exeter.   Looking at the site today it is hard to realise that during the Second World War it was here, in an underground Sector Operations Room, that aircraft of the RAF's No.10 Group Fighter Command were effectively controlled. Their role was the defence of the South West skies and protection of cities such as Bristol and Cardiff as well as the defence of vital naval bases at Plymouth and Portland. In addition they provided aerial cover for vital supply convoys using English Channel and, later, as the war progressed, the D-Day landings in Normandy.

12

No.10 Group Fighter Command's Sector Control Room at RAF Poltimore in 1942

Summing up some of the operations covered by RAF Poltimore is former Spitfire pilot Roy Hook, now an octogenarian living at Exmouth, who in January 1943 served with No. 602 Squadron at RAF Perranporth on the North Cornwall coast. He recalls:

"During the next few months we were sent on a wide range of missions, many of which were routine. These included scrambling to chase off enemy intruders probing our airspace and providing defensive cover for the vital supply convoys as they left the South West Approaches to sail up the English Channel. I also flew a number of missions escorting Flying Fortresses whilst they attacked enemy naval targets at Brest, on Brittany's Atlantic Coast, and also escorted the smaller Venturas to attack strategic targets at Cherbourg and St. Brieuc. However, the most exciting were the fighter sweeps we carried out over Brittany and Normandy and the low-level shipping reconnaissance flights we carried out close to the coast between the Isle of Batz and Ushant."

During the build up to D-Day and in the days which followed Poltimore remained as busy as ever, in theory being the closest Sector Control to the invasion beaches. However, as the Allies advanced further into Europe, Poltimore's front-line importance diminished and the RAF finally left the building in 1946. However this was not quite the end of Poltimore's role in the nation's defence. It was subsequently taken over by the Royal Observer Corps as the new Headquarters for their No. 10 Group.

We were now entering the era of the 'Cold War' and the threat from the nuclear weapons of the Soviet Eastern Bloc. The role of the ROC had dramatically changed too; gone were the cliff-top spotting posts looking out for enemy aircraft. These were replaced by more sophisticated, yet operationally simple, underground bunkers with equipment capable of locating nuclear bomb bursts and, more importantly, tracking their potentially deadly radio-active fall-out. To facilitate the ROC's new role a number of semi-nuclear proof operations centres were built across Britain and it is one of these which can still be seen at Poltimore today. It was equipped with its own power and an air supply protected against nuclear contamination. Entry to the building was only through heavy steel doors and an air-lock. Today it remains as a legacy from the 'Cold War' whilst the WW II Sector Control Room still lies underground beneath the single storey huts which, at the time of writing, are to the left of the main building.

Had a nuclear attack been made on Britain teams of observers, numbering around a hundred in all, would have been capable of monitoring the nuclear fall-out situation for 24 hours a day and for many days. During this period the Group's parent RAF Station was RAF St. Mawgan in Cornwall. However, with the eventual demise of Soviet power, and the rapprochement which followed, the nuclear threat passed and as part of the 'peace dividend' the ROC was disbanded at the end of 1991. The Home Office then occupied the site for a few years before putting it up for sale and an uncertain future.

RAF EXMINSTER

This small RAF Station, set in the Exminster Marshes and only a handful of miles from the centre of Exeter, was to play an important role in the defence of the city. It owed its existence to one of the most significant inventions of WWII - Radar, an acronym for Radio Detecting and Ranging which detected the approach of enemy aircraft. By modern standards these early systems were extremely basic and to facilitate adequate coverage a relatively large number of radar stations were required. These soon sprung up along the south and east coasts and amongst these early installations was another at Branscombe, between Sidmouth and Seaton. Known as Chain Home Stations, their early warning systems suffered a number of limitations.

However improvements were made and after RAF Exminster was opened in 1941 many advances in technology became available. These included a new Ground Controlled Interception system , shortened to GCI. Now plotters could not only detect incoming enemy aircraft but take the appropriate defensive counter-measures. In fact Exminster has been described as a classic GCI station with its 'ops' room referred to as the 'happy drome'! However, its role must not be confused with that of near-by RAF Poltimore.

As previously described. Poltimore was the Sector Control for No.10 Group Fighter Command and had responsibility for air operations throughout the SW Peninsula and for aircraft making sweeps across the Channel. Exminster's role was purely local defence and almost invariably the only aircraft they controlled were those based at nearby RAF Exeter. However, together with other similar stations, they also fed information into Poltimore, a factor which served to enhance their important link in the defensive chain.

Like many hastily built RAF stations, the early occupants were billeted with local families, mainly in and around the village of Exminster although some lived in Topsham and had to be ferried across the Exe for duty. Later 'official' accommodation was provided in Nissen huts built in the Clifton Hill area of Exeter, the duty crews being bussed to and from the Exminster site.

The station also had a secondary role, that of housing the local Observer Corps HQ. This had been at Barnfield Hall in Exeter but was destroyed during the blitz. As a result the RAF accommodated the Corps until they were able to move into the premises vacated by the RAF at Poltimore.

Post-war, RAF Exminster provided facilities for Fighter Controllers of the Royal Auxiliary Air Force's No.3512 County of Devon Fighter Control Unit whose main HQ was at RAF Rose Duryard. However their dependence on Exminster ceased when facilities at RAF Hope Cove were updated. Training was switched to Hope Cove and ultimately RAF Exminster was put on 'care and maintenance'. By late 1957 political changes heralded the closure of the R.Aux.A.F. Fighter Control Units which were completed by 1958. Their former HQ at Rose Duryard now lies within the campus of Exeter University.

The RAF disposed of Exminster in 1959 when private enterprise moved in and the site was later renamed Lion's Rest Estate after a bedding factory which was established there. Interestingly, Grahame Holloway, the author of this book, was familiar with the lay-out of the station having visited it whilst serving as Intelligence and Security Officer with No.3512 FCU. This was a factor which proved valuable when, later serving as a police officer, in 1959 he was called to a double murder at the factory. But, as they say, that is another story !

RAF EXETER

Arguably, the RAF's most important base in the South West during WWII was at Exeter. Already a civilian airfield before the war it was quickly commandeered by the RAF in September 1939 when a research team moved in from Farnborough to undertake trials on the most effective way to destroy barrage balloon cables. However civilian flights were still maintained, primarily to Channel Islands by Jersey Airlines until they became occupied by the enemy in June 1940. Shortly afterwards, on the 6th July 1940, RAF Exeter was officially commissioned and construction work started on additional buildings although at this stage the grass runways still remained.

However the first operational squadrons had already arrived prior to commissioning with the first, No. 213 Squadron equipped with Hurricanes, arriving in June. This was closely followed on the 5th July by further Hurricanes of No. 87 Squadron. The pilots of both these squadrons were already battle hardened veterans having provided aerial cover during the evacuation from Dunkirk. Subsequently both were to play an important role during the Battle of Britain.

1941 saw many changes at Exeter when the first Polish Squadron arrived. This was No. 307, a night fighter squadron which was initially equipped with Boulton Paul Defiants. However these were later replaced by Beaufighters and Mosquitoes. A second Polish Squadron, No. 317, also arrived in 1941. They were equipped with Hurricanes and remained until the following year.

More frantic activity came when the contractors returned to replace the airfield's grass runways with three concrete ones in the now familiar pattern. Their completion saw Exeter's operational commitments increase dramatically, occupying as it did a strategic position in the South West. Other squadrons were soon to arrive and the list of

17

various types to operate from the base grew rapidly. Records show that almost thirty different squadrons operated out of Exeter at various times bringing with them a great variety of aircraft. In addition to those already mentioned others included Typhoons, Tempests, Whirlwinds and light bombers such as the Havoc and Ventura. Then there was the Lysander, surreptitiously used for clandestine operations with the French Underground where its short landing and take-off capabilities were invaluable. The list continues for the Royal Navy occasionally flew their Swordfish from here whilst another maritime aircraft seen was the Walrus which performed a valuable air-sea rescue role.

Whirlwinds of Exeter based No.263 Squadron. 1940 - 41

RAF Exeter also performed another vital role during the early years of the war when the destruction of the U-boat pens along France's Atlantic coast became vital to prevent the destruction of convoys bringing in essential supplies by sea. The RAF suffered many casualties during raids on these heavily defended targets and others in occupied Europe Often those severely damaged and struggling to make the homeward flight with a wounded crew would see the coast of Devon and aim for a safe landing at Exeter. Initially most of these aircraft were light to medium bombers such as the Whitley, Blenheim and Wellington but by 1943-44 the airfield saw the arrival of larger crippled

crippled aircraft such as the Halifax and Lancaster. Sadly, records show that many of these crews perished in sight of the airfield.

The Hawker Tempest, one of the types of aircraft based at RAF Exeter during WWII

Early 1944 saw a dramatic change at RAF Exeter when the Americans arrived. Although not aware of it at the time, the assault on mainland Europe and the D-day landings were already being formulated and Exeter was one of the nearest bases to the proposed Normandy landing grounds. RAF squadrons were relocated to other bases as the build up of American forces continued.

Eventually RAF Exeter became 'Station 463' of the USAAF and the temporary home of the USAAF 50th Troop Carrier Wing. This comprised the 440th Troop Carrier Group with four squadrons of C-47 carrier aircraft, known within the RAF as the Dakota. With gliders in tow these were to play an important role on D-day, dropping airborne troops on the Cherbourg Peninsula. Once the bridgehead had been secured they reverted to their transport role, ferrying supplies out and bringing the wounded home.

Although still an American base, the RAF continued to fly from here when it was deemed operationally expedient. Such flights included low level intruder missions by the Mosquitoes of No. 51 Squadron.

When hostilities finally ended in 1945, as with many other airfields, the RAF had no further use for Exeter and so facilities were withdrawn to the Service's permanent bases elsewhere. On the 1st January 1947 the airfield was officially returned to the Ministry of Civil Aviation. However, interestingly, this did not spell the complete end of RAF operations.

There was still a need for the continuation training of the reserve forces and in 1949 the airfield became home to the RAF's No. 10 Reserve Flying School. Originally equipped with Tiger Moths, Ansons and Oxfords, these were later phased out with the arrival of the then new basic trainer, the Chipmunk. These operated until government expenditure cut-backs closed the unit in 1954.

Despite the closure of No. 10 RFS, RAF aircraft continued to fly out of Exeter until the mid-1990's due to two completely different types of operation. Firstly, it became home to No. 3. Civilian Anti-Aircraft Co-operation Unit (CAACU) in March 1951, a hybrid unit equipped with 'end of service' RAF aircraft which were flown by reservists in a civilian capacity and maintained under a civilian contract. Duties included providing 'fighter interception' exercises to train RAF Fighter Controllers, towing target drogues for naval gunnery practice or simulated air attacks on exercising troops.

Two members of the East Devon Branch of the AirCrew Association, Ted King and Max Pattison, were both CAACU pilots at one stage of their flying careers. Max summed up the experience as being the *"best of both worlds; the thrills of service flying without the red tape and restrictions of service life."*

20

Balliols of No.3 CAACU, Exeter, in a 'fighter interception' role. 1957

By the time CAACU closed in 1971 its pilots had flown at various times, Oxfords, Beaufighters, Spitfires, Ansons, Balliols and Mosquitoes. Later, converting to jets, it operated at various periods the single-seat Vampire, Hunter, Meteor 7 and Vampire T11.

The second unit to occupy a site at the airport was the RAF's No. 4 Air Experience Flight which, equipped with Chipmunks, provided an introduction to flying for many thousands of West Country Air Training Corps Cadets. It closed in the mid- 1990's ending over fifty years of an RAF presence at Exeter Airport. A number of members of the East Devon Branch of the AirCrew Association served as instructors over the years. These included 'Dickie' Dougan who was its CO between 1965-68, Bernard Greenaway who is currently Chairman of Exmouth RAFA Club and John Durrant who it is estimated flew some 4000 cadets during his service with the unit.

RAF DUNKESWELL.

Situated atop the Blackdown Hills in East Devon, close to the border with Somerset, lies Dunkeswell Airfield. Still used commercially, albeit on a minor scale, its long concrete runways remain in place and there is a miscellany of buildings which house a cafe and control tower in support of a local flying club and use as a parachuting centre. However, its ambience today bears little relationship to the frenetic activity here between 1941-45.

With an urgent requirement for additional airfields, work on RAF Dunkeswell started in 1941 when a large number of Irish navvies moved on site to work for the main contractors, George Whimpy. As well as the necessary infrastructure, their work included the laying of three concrete runways to the conventional design. The site officially opened as RAF Dunkeswell in early 1942 when it was allocated for use by RAF No. 10 Group Fighter Command. Unfortunately work had fallen behind schedule and with changing operational needs its intended use was switched from Fighter Command to Coastal Command with the proposed arrival of three squadrons of maritime aircraft from No. 19 Group.

In 1942 the 'Battle of the Atlantic' was at its height and the necessity for maritime patrol aircraft was a high priority. However despite this the contractor's workforce allowed the work to fall even further behind schedule with the result that, although officially 'operational', hardly any use was made of the base during the year. Fortunately a dramatic change was to occur in July 1943. This was the month the Americans arrived and RAF Dunkeswell was quickly transformed into an air base for the United States Navy. Destined to become the home of their No. 7 Air Wing, it was their only land base in the UK and developed into their largest in Europe.

In fact the first operational aircraft to arrive were not naval but Liberators of USAAF 479th Anti-submarine Group which until then had been operating out of RAF St.Eval in Cornwall. However, with the subsequent arrival of the US navy the early model Liberators were replaced by the PB4Y-1, a specialised anti-submarine version which was painted in a distinctive blue/grey livery.

Joining the navy's Liberators at Dunkeswell were a number of other types which included a detachment of Catalinas, which were used for reconnaissance and air-sea rescue missions, a couple of Vultee Vengeances and a flight of six Spitfires. The latter were allocated to the Royal Navy but operated by the Americans under Royal Navy markings. The facilities at Dunkeswell also continued to be occasionally used by USAAF B-17 Flying Fortresses as a diversionary base.

Those paying a nostalgic visit to the former air base will find a memorial has been erected to those who served there. Incorporating a propeller, the poignant dedication reads: *"Many returned home, some stayed forever, none will be forgotten"*

However today's visitor should also visit the nearby parish church. Here they will find an 'American corner' where a Roll of Honour contains the names of those who paid the ultimate sacrifice. Amongst those recorded there is Lt. Joseph Kennedy, elder brother of the late J.F.Kennedy, President of the United States. In the eighteen months of operations from Dunkeswell, the US Navy's 7th Air Wing lost a total of twenty-nine aircraft in combat, in many cases with a complete loss of crew.

As the war in Europe ended the US Navy wasted no time in withdrawing from Dunkeswell and by the end of July 1945 they had departed. On the 6th August 1945 the base was transferred to RAF Transport Command's No.46 Group. It became engaged in a number of minor tasks, including ferrying operations, but by March 1946 most of these commitments had been fulfilled and the station was down-graded to 'care and maintenance'.   The RAF finally relinquished control in February 1949.

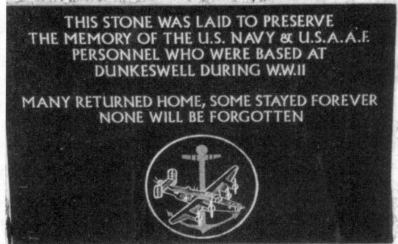

THIS STONE WAS LAID TO PRESERVE
THE MEMORY OF THE U.S. NAVY & U.S.A.A.F.
PERSONNEL WHO WERE BASED AT
DUNKESWELL DURING W.W.II

MANY RETURNED HOME, SOME STAYED FOREVER
NONE WILL BE FORGOTTEN

The Dunkeswell Memorial and its dedication to the US Forces.

RAF UPOTTERY (SMEATHARPE)

Also situated in East Devon in the area of the Blackdown Hills is the former RAF Station at Upottery which was known locally as RAF Smeatharpe after the small village adjacent to its eastern perimeter. It was actually quite a late entrant as far as the war effort was concerned for although construction work commenced in the Spring of 1943 it was not officially opened until February 1944, barely 4 months before D-day.

Originally placed under Control of RAF 70 Group it was, nevertheless, intended for use by medium bombers such as the B-25 Mitchell and B-26 Marauder operated by the USAAF. When the Americans eventually arrived in April 1944 the base officially became USAAF Station No.462. However the expected bombers did not materialise.

D-day was less than eight weeks away and the Allies' operational requirements were now completely different. Four squadrons of Douglas C-47 Skytrains (known to the RAF as the Dakota) and C-53 Skytroopers arrived as part of the USAAF 439th Troop Carrier Group and the larger 50th Wing of the US Troop Carrier Command. These were joined by Horsa and Waco gliders as the build-up for the assault on occupied Europe gathered pace and training at the base intensified.

Above: The Horsa Glider

25

However, Upottery was not alone in experiencing such activity. Exeter was experiencing a similar build-up whist in Somerset the 50th US Troop Carrier Command was expanding its operations at Merryfield and Weston Zoyland.

The story of this great event was later to become the subject of an epic motion picture. *'The Longest Day'* which starred actors from both sides of the Atlantic. Of these Hollywood legend John Wayne played the part of Colonel Charles Young, the Commander of the US 101st Airborne Division whose paratroops landed on the Cherbourg Peninsula and liberated the French town of St. Mere Eglise   In reality Colonel Young and his men were conveyed to their dropping zone, and moment in history, from Upottery in a fleet of eighty aircraft.

With the bridgehead in Normandy successfully established, the USAAF had no further use for Upottery and the RAF regained control in August 1944 with the last of the troop-carriers departing the following month. However at the end of the year the Americans returned again, albeit as a temporary measure, when the runways at their Dunkeswell base were being re-surfaced. Although this presence remained the base was now officially part of RAF No. 19 Group Coastal Command. Both the RAF and the US Navy operated Liberators from the base, their main sphere of operations being the Bay of Biscay where the hunt for enemy U-boats continued.

The Americans left the base in July 1945 to return to the United States but as the war ended the RAF, too, had no further use for it and it passed to the care of Maintenance Command. It finally closed in November 1948 when the land was returned to the local farmer.

Although no longer fulfilling any aviation use many reminders of its former wartime role are still evident. Large tracts of runway are plainly visible whilst elsewhere one can see dilapidated remains of various huts, the former control tower and, perhaps most interesting of all, a squat tower-like building once used to train bomb-aimers.

Upottery today.
Left: The bomb aimers'
training tower.
Below: The control tower

Another chapter in the life of RAF Upottery was written on the 6th June 2005, the 61st anniversary of D-day, when a memorial was unveiled in honour of those who left the airfield for the D-day assault but lost their lives during the course of the operation.

Left: The Upottery Memorial.

It is situated off the airfield, close to the village of Smeatharpe at Moonhayes Cross.

It is attached to one of the few remaining sentry boxes which once guarded the approach roads to the airfield.

The inscription on the tablet reads:

Upottery - USAAF Station 462

Just after midnight on the 5th June 1944, 81 C-47 unarmed transport aircraft departed from this airfield carrying 1357 Paratroops who were to be dropped behind enemy lines near the coast of France on D-Day.

At dawn on the morning of 7th June, 50 C-47 aircraft towing 30 Horsa gliders and 20 Waco gliders departed for France carrying 968 Glider Infantry Troops in the second airborne wave of the Invasion.

Here in honoured memory are those killed on those two missions.

The memorial then lists the names of all the fallen under their appropriate units, the 439th Troop Carrier Group USAAF, the 506th Parachute Infantry Regiment of the 101st Airborne Division US Army and the 325th Glider Infantry Regiment 82nd Airborne Division US Army.

The Douglas C-47 - known by the RAF as the Dakota.

A WACO glider

RNAS HALDON - HMS HERON II

Situated on the top of the Haldon Hills, and occupying an area part of which is now used by the Teignmouth Golf Club, is the former Haldon airfield. It has a long history which certainly dates from the early pioneer days of aviation for records show that in 1928 an Avro 594 Avian was purchased by William Parkhouse, the then airfield owner who went on to manage Exeter Airport. At that time the airfield was used mainly for events such as 'Flying Circuses' or 'Air Pageants'.

A brief period as a commercial airfield followed in the Spring of 1933 when a small airline, known as GWR Air Services, started a twice-weekly service between Plymouth's Roborough airfield and Cardiff, with an interim stop at Haldon. They had one aircraft, a Westland Wessex, which was chartered from Imperial Airways. The following year Provincial Airways included a Haldon stop on their route from Croydon to Plymouth via Southampton. Their aircraft was the De Havilland Dragon, a forerunner of the Rapide.

During the pre-war period the grass field was also occasionally used by military aircraft undertaking various trials such as those involving landing aids. Two types seen at Haldon were the Fairey IIIF and the Vickers Virginia, the latter being probably the largest aircraft ever to land there having been designed for the RAF as a heavy night bomber. Entering RAF service in 1924, this huge bi-plane was powered by two Napier engines giving it a top speed of 108 mph and a capability of carrying a bomb load of 3000 lbs. Surprisingly some Virginias were still flying as late as 1941 !

Shortly after the outbreak of WWII the Royal Navy saw the merits of having a coastal airfield and requisitioned it from its owner for Fleet Air Arm use. As is the naval tradition it became a 'ship' and was designated HMS Heron II. Although now having control of the airfield, the navy did not take up any tangible occupation until August 1941 when detachments were made from its parent station at Yeovilton. Most of the activity comprised target-towing aircraft from 761 and 794 Squadrons. However operational requirements proved minimal and in May 1943 the base was reduced to Care and Maintenance status.

Post war the site returned to private ownership and by the late 1960's part was once again being used by golfers, the rest reverting to scrub. Today, other than the remains of the former club house located amid the scrub near Little Haldon Cross, you would be hard pushed to find any tangible evidence of its early flying history. However, this is not to say it has been forgotten for a simple plaque set in a granite block records those early days and will be found in the car park on the East side of the main road .

One member of the East Devon Branch who can recollect its early naval use is Dick Allen of Exton. Returning to the UK after completing his flying training in the United States, he was posted to No. 762 Fighter Training Squadron based at RNAS, Yeovilton, which was also known as HMS Heron. The squadron flew Fairey Fulmars and at the end of December 1942 Dick arrived at Haldon to serve a short detachment whilst undertaking gunnery training off Teignmouth.

Asked to recall the facilities and any incidents during his detachment at Haldon, Dick replied..

"The facilities were extremely limited, nothing more than a few huts. Fortunately, as aircrew, we were looked after quite well and were billeted in a large hotel at the end of Teignmouth Sea Front from where we were taken to the airfield by bus each morning. As for incidents there were none really because our flying was basically

a continuation of weapons training.   However we did have one notable event although not involving any of our aircraft. An American Army Air Force squadron of P-38 Lightnings was being re-deployed from a base somewhere in Southern England to a destination in North Africa and following a flight path which took them close to the French coast.   To avoid German radar they were flying at sea level when one of the aircraft struck the sea, losing a propeller.   Leaving the others, it returned across the Channel on one engine when, for some reason, the pilot decided to land at Haldon.   To be honest it was travelling at some speed and with the airfield being so small we didn't think the pilot would make it.   However, we hadn't reckoned on the aircraft's tricycle undercarriage which was fairly new to us. As soon as he touched down the pilot slammed on the brakes and, to our amazement, the aircraft came to a rapid halt.   Other than that my short stay at the airfield was relatively excitement free. "

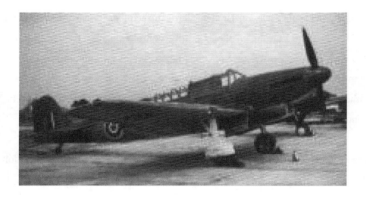

The Fulmar, pictured above, entered squadron service in June 1940 and was the first 8-gun fighter to be operated by the Royal Navy, its armament giving it the same fire-power as the Spitfire and Hurricane. Although powered by a Rolls Royce Merlin VIII engine, its larger size and two-man crew meant its top speed was only 256 mph.   It was also no match in other respects.

| AIRCRAFT | | PILOT, OR 1ST PILOT | 2 |
Type	No.		
Fulmar	N 401	Self	
Martlett	b.J. 511	Self	
"	b.J. 555	Self	
Fulmar II	4093	Self	
"	1925	Self	
"	4093	Self	
"	8732	Self	
"	8732	Self	
"	1925	Self	
"	4093	Self	

An extract from Dick Allen's log book showing entries for
December 1942 in which he flew a Fairey Fulmar from Haldon.

After Haldon Dick became known as a Wildcat 'ace'. Flying the robust Grumman
Wildcat from carriers, he was twice awarded the DSC for exploits whilst operating in
areas ranging from the Bay of Biscay and the Arctic whilst in defence of the Russian
convoys.

Reminders of Haldon Airfield. Top, the memorial and, below,
the chimney of the old club house.

RAF BOLT HEAD

RAF Bolt Head was one of a number of small rudimentary airfields to be constructed along the coast with the aim of giving aircraft operating from there a shorter distance to their target areas and, consequently, a longer time to attack the enemy. It was situated on a cliff-top site close to the small resort of Salcombe in the South Hams area of the County and opened in 1941 as a Forward Operating Base (FOB) for fighter squadrons from Nos.10 and 11 Groups. Their primary role was the escort of bombers attacking strategic targets in Western France and, although never a major airfield, records show that during its four years of wartime operations no fewer that fourteen squadrons deployed aircraft from here, albeit not at the same time. Interestingly, the first aircraft to be permanently based there were two Lysanders detached from No. 276 Squadron.

The following year, 1942, as operational deployments increased, extra facilities were provided. These included blister hangars, two 'Sommerfield' track runways and bulk fuel storage together with barracks, flight and office accommodation. Unfortunately this work was spotted by the Luftwaffe who attacked with two Messerschmitt Bf 109's on March 7th and hit a No.317 Squadron Spitfire as it was taking off. Luckily the pilot managed to land unhurt. It was given satellite status in the April of that year although it continued to be used as a FOB by the Exeter based squadrons when engaged in escort or fighter sweep (Rhubarb) roles.

The largest aircraft to operate from the station were Bostons from No.2 Group Bomber Command which used it as a base to bomb such targets as Morlaix on the 30th March 1942, although the Luftwaffe retaliated the next day with four Bf 109's which damaged a number of Spitfires. Activity from Bolt Head intensified greatly prior to and during the Normandy landings when the main aircraft operating strikes from here were the Typhoon, Spitfire and, occasionally, the Mosquito.

The station's closeness to the sea also gave rise to another role, that of Air Sea Rescue. Whilst ASR Spitfires would make sweeps to locate ditched aircrew the aircraft itself had no means of effecting a rescue. That task would fall to either high speed launches or amphibious aircraft such as the Supermarine Walrus operated by No.276 Squadron from Bolt Head during 1944.

Left: The largest aircraft known to have used Bolt Head is the US Built Douglas Boston

Right. The ASR Walrus

Known affectionately by its crews as the 'Shagbat', the Walrus was fitted with a Bristol Pegasus engine mounted as a rearwards facing 'pusher' between the bi-plane's wings. Its top speed was given as 135 mph and it cruised at 95 mph.   Interestingly, the prototype was designed by RJ Mitchell who is better known as the designer of the Spitfire.

As war ended, Bolt Head was reduced to Care & Maintenance status at the end of April 1945 and finally closed two years later. Today the airfield has reverted back to farmland. The remains of a few buildings may be seen together with a small strip of the former access track.

RAF ROBOROUGH (Plymouth)

Now Plymouth City Airport, this was a small grass airfield situated to the North East of the City adjacent to the road to Yelverton (see entry on RAF Harrowbeer). Pre-war it provided facilities for pleasure flights and later, circa 1935, became the terminus for the route flown by Provincial Airways from Croydon. However with outbreak of war, and the large naval base located at nearby Devonport, the field was hastily requisitioned by the Royal Navy for use by No. 2 Anti-aircraft Co-operation Unit.

In 1940, with the defence of the naval base of paramount importance, it was switched to use as a fighter airfield. One of the earliest aircraft to arrive was a flight of Gloster Gladiators belonging to No. 247 Squadron. This remarkable single-seat bi-plane, with a top speed of over 250 mph, first entered service in February 1937 and, although already obsolete by the time war was declared, remained in front line service throughout the Battle of Britain and the defence of Malta. However, one of its main roles from Roborough was patrolling the coast for any unusual activities which could foretell an enemy landing, the invasion scare being at its height at this time. This was carried out in conjunction with its other role of Air-Sea Rescue.

A detachment of No. 247 Squadron Hurricanes briefly operated from the airfield during the early months of 1941 but moved to RAF Portreath in May of that year. A year later, in May 1942, the airfield officially transferred from the Royal Navy to RAF control, the change making little difference to the operations of No.2 AACU. Their 'A' Flight became 1623 Flight in February 1943 and continued to use various types of aircraft for gun-laying exercises. These included the Gladiator, Defiant, Fairey Battle and, at one stage, two Barracudas. In December, 1943, 1623 Flight became No. 691 Squadron and operated Hurricanes and Oxfords for similar exercises. Other units using the airfield included No. 19 Group Communications Flight which operated the Anson.

Above: The Gladiator operated from RAF Roborough by No.247 Squadron in 1940

However, perhaps Roborough's most memorable incident came in August 1941 when a USAAF B-17 Flying Fortress, severely damaged by seven Bf 109's whilst on a raid on Brest, attempted an emergency landing.   One engine was on fire and its flaps and ailerons were inoperative. Sadly the field was too small and it overran, hitting a tank trap and bursting into flames.

As the war in Europe neared its end, military activity at Roborough declined and civil flying restarted in 1946. However, around 1960 the Royal Navy returned with Tiger Moths, later replacing them with Chipmunks. These formed an Air Experience Flight for the naval cadets at Britannia Royal Naval College, Dartmouth, and were operated under contract by Airwork.   In 1967 the Air Troop of 41 Commando, Royal Marines, used Roborough as a base for a small number of Sioux helicopters which were later temporarily joined by three Sioux from the Air Troop of No. 95 Commando Light Regiment of the Royal Artillery. They all left in 1972 when the Royal Marines moved to their base at Coypool.   Today the airfield still lacks facilities to handle large aircraft and commercially remains in the shadow of its much larger neighbour at Exeter.

38

RAF HARROWBEER

Situated on the western fringe of the Dartmoor National Park, close to the village of Yelverton, Harrowbeer first opened as an RAF Station in August 1941. It was initially designated as a fighter station under the control of No.10 Group Fighter Command and a satellite of RAF Exeter.

During its period as a military airfield some seventeen different squadrons operated from Harrowbeer, including a couple from the Fleet Air Arm. In addition to the British, pilots from six other nations also flew from here. These included Canadians, Rhodesians, Poles, Czechs, French and Americans. One of the first squadrons to arrive was the RAF's No 130 Squadron which operated Spitfire MkV's as escorts to bomber raids and also on shipping patrols. However their stay was a short one, only the months of October and November, before being deployed elsewhere. Then there were the Spitfires flown by No. 302 (Polish) Squadron and No. 312 (Czech) Squadron. Other aircraft operating from the airfield included the Hurricane which made a brief appearance in 1942 when No.175 Squadron was based there .

By late 1942, however, it was changing from a predominantly fighter base to that of a more versatile fighter-bomber role engaged on anti-shipping strikes. It also saw the arrival of Typhoons of No. 193 Squadron which undertook a variety of roles which included the interception of Luftwaffe 'intruder' patrols as well as making their own sweeps on predominately rail and airfield targets in Northern France. In early 1943 the Typhoons were joined by Whirlwinds of No. 263 Squadron which re-located from Exeter. By now the Harrowbeer based squadrons had another vital role - attacking the newly constructed V-1 sites in Northern France.

With its proximity to the Channel, Harrowbeer also acquired another important task, that of Air Sea Rescue. These sweeps to locate 'downed' aircrew were usually undertaken by the older model Spitfires such as the MkIII flown by No.276 Squadron during 1941-44.

A Typhoon similar to those flown by No.193 Squadron at RAF Harrowbeer in 1943. Its four 20 mm Hispano cannon are clearly visible.

Following D-day, and with the Allied advance through France firmly established, the base was temporarily reduced to Care & Maintenance status although it still remained open for operational flying by Communications Flight aircraft. However in January 1945 it reopened for more extensive use by fighter squadron detachments, Anti-Aircraft Co-operation Units and, in late 1947, by No. 19 Group Communications Flight which transferred from Roborough.

Eventually the RAF vacated the airfield in the Summer of 1948 following which there was a heated debate as to its future use. Many saw the large concrete runways providing a sound base for a new airport for the City of Plymouth. The Ministry of Civil Aviation put forward proposals but these raised strong opposition from conservationists. Their argument was based on the fact the airfield had been constructed within the Dartmoor National Park and therefore should revert to its natural state as common land. In the end the conservationists won the day.

Today the former airfield is a popular leisure area comprising a mix of gorse and moorland pasture. However remnants of its historic role during WWII still remain and sections of runway are clearly visible together with the perimeter track. Here many of the aircraft dispersal bays have been preserved and those using the access road behind the 'Leg 'O Mutton Inn' will find a granite memorial to those who served there.

The Harrowbeer Memorial. It's inscription reads as follows:
" RAF Harrowbeer.   Operational 1941 - 1949.

From this station flew pilots of many Commonwealth and Allied countries, including Britain, Canada, Czechoslovakia, France, Poland, Southern   Rhodesia   and   the USA, with the support of the ground crews and airfield defence units.   This stone is in memory of all those who served here and especially those who gave their lives. Many local residents helped build and maintain this airfield.   Unveiled by the first Station Commander, Group Captain the Hon E.F. Ward on the 15th August 1981, the fortieth anniversary of the opening of this station.

RAF OKEHAMPTON (Folly Gate).

The wild moorland of Dartmoor has long provided a training ground for the military so it is perhaps not surprising to find an airfield existed on level ground close to its northern fringe . This was just north of Okehampton, adjoining the eastern side of the A386 main road to Hatherleigh. Basically it stretched from the village of Folly Gate as far as the junction with the first, now unclassified, road into Okehampton.

It is known the field existed pre-war when it was used as an Army Co-operation base. Subsequent to the outbreak of hostilities its use was slowly expanded and there is a record that in August 1940 a reformed No.16 Squadron arrived with their Lysanders having received severe casualties whilst operating in France. On arrival they commenced dawn and dusk coastal patrols over an area covering the Bristol Channel from Barnstaple to Portishead and also, to the South, Lyme Bay. Their role was to search for any suspicious movements. By late Autumn the notoriously fickle Dartmoor weather was making itself felt and the unit redeployed to Harrowbeer.

Eventually it became a satellite of Weston Zoyland in May 1941 but it was never a major airfield and from March 1942 was used by No.73 Maintenance Unit for holding spares, although occasional use continued by Army Co-operation detachments and also Piper Cubs flown by the US Army. The main aircraft to use the airfield were Lysanders and Austers. Some locals maintain that the field was also used as an explosives store.

Never other than a grass field, today the land has been returned to private ownership and is currently used as pasture. It is left largely to one's imagination as to the field's facilities although locals graphically describe how Nissen huts once stood where the row of houses facing the main road now stand. However according to local information, there is one legacy remaining and that is the Folly Gate village hall. Since enlarged and improved, it incorporates the former NAAFI.

Folly Gate Village Hall incorporating the one-time NAAFI.

With help one may find the odd reminder, such as a concrete hut base, but these are on private land so perhaps the best reason for visiting the area is to stand at a gate and enjoy the distant view of Dartmoor!

Two of the aircraft which operated from Folly Gate between 1939-1942

Top: A Lysander used for patrolling the Bristol Channel and Lyme Bay.

Bottom: An Army Air Corps Auster used for artillery spotting exercises on Dartmoor.

RAF MOUNT BATTEN

The City of Plymouth has an exceptionally long and enviable military tradition. History records its role with Drake and the Spanish Armada, its staunch support for Parliament during the civil war and the large citadel erected by Charles II when the monarchy was restored as a warning to its citizens not to do so again. In more recent times it has become one of our most important naval bases, the wide estuary of the Tamar and the waters of Plymouth Sound providing an ideal anchorage. The giant naval dockyard at Devonport has produced some of our finest warships. The Royal Marines are also much in evidence, both at barracks within the city and their Commando base on the outskirts at Bickleigh. With such history it is not surprising that the Royal Air Force should eventually find a niche there too.

However it was not the RAF which first recognised that, as well as a haven for shipping, the waters of Plymouth Sound also provided safe moorings for seaplanes and amphibious aircraft. This honour goes to the Royal Navy which saw the potential as long ago as the First World War when they opened a base on the city outskirts at Cattedown where the River Plym flows into the Sound. Known as RNAS Cattedown, it is recorded they operated small airships and fixed-wing aircraft from here, primarily in reconnaissance and anti-submarine patrols. One notable milestone came at the end of May 1919 when the base was the finishing point for the historic Atlantic crossing made by a NC-4 flying boat of the US Navy.

The navy continued to use the base until it was transferred to the Royal Air Force and renamed RAF Mount Batten on the 1st October 1929. In the years which followed the RAF operated various types of seaplane from their new base until the start of WWII. These included Supermarine's Southampton and Scapa, and the London built by Saunders-Roe. The first of these, the Southampton, dated from 1925 when it was based at Calshot and made many record-breaking long -distance flights, notably a

45

27,000 mile 'cruise' of the Far East in 1927. It entered service with No. 204 Squadron at Mount Batten at about the time the RAF took over the base.

An early 1930's Supermarine Southampton
operated by No.204 Squadron based at RAF Mount Batten.

These early seaplanes were later replaced by another Supermarine aircraft, the Scapa which made its maiden flight in 1932 and first entered service in the UK with No. 204 Squadron at Mount Batten in August 1935. The aircraft was powered by two 525 hp Kestrel engines which gave it a top speed of 141 mph at 3000 feet. Of all-metal construction it carried a crew of five. It was eventually withdrawn from front-line squadron service in 1938.

In the meanwhile 204 Squadron's Southamptons were replaced in October 1936 by the even newer Saro London. Powered by two 1000 hp Bristol Pegasus engines it had a top speed of 155 mph at 6,250 feet and cruised at 129 mph. It had a nominal range in excess of 1000 miles which could be extended by use of a long-range fuel tank. At outbreak of war the RAF had twenty-nine Londons still in service, those based in Gibraltar remaining operational until 1941.

Not surprisingly, it will be for the Short Sunderland which RAF Mount Batten will be best remembered. This giant four-engine flying boat first entered RAF service in 1938 and, serving with distinction throughout WWII, went on to become the RAF's longest ever serving front-line aircraft. Subsequently seeing service during the Berlin Airlift, in Korea and against insurgents in Malaysia it remained at the forefront of RAF operations until finally retired from front-line service in 1959 .

However, No. 204 Squadron was not the only one to operate from Mount Batten during the war. Others included Nos. 10, 95, 210 461 and No.2 AACU. Of these it has been said that most remembered will be No. 10 Squadron of the Royal Australian Air Force. Part of No. 19 Group RAF Coastal Command, their Sunderland aircraft flew no fewer than 3,177 sorties over the often hostile waters of the Bay of Biscay and the Western Approaches of the Atlantic Ocean. However their tally of seven U-boats definitely sunk was not achieved without great loss. A total of nineteen Sunderlands were lost to enemy action and a further six destroyed in flying accidents. The war over, the crews of No. 10 Squadron returned home to Australia in October 1945.

RAF Mount Batten continued as a base for some years after the war although, with the eventual withdrawal of the Sunderland, flying operations ceased . However another role should not be overlooked, that of Air Sea Rescue. The RAF's Marine Branch operated its high-speed launches from here for many years and when post-war its rescue role diminished the launches were used for towing targets. Major maintenance for all the Units vessels was also carried out locally.

The Short Sunderland.

As well as being used extensively during WWII the Sunderland was one of the very few aircraft flown operationally by the RAF during the Korean War.   Later variants were equipped with four 1200 hp Pratt & Whitney Twin Wasp engines.

Mount Batten also operated the RAF School of Combat Survival and Rescue for aircrew and with its coastal position much emphasis of its training was on sea survival. Arguably, one of it most important peace-time roles was acting as the Maritime Headquarters and Air Sea Rescue Co-ordination Centre.   Here rescues over a large proportion of the Western Hemisphere were co-ordinated but when the RAF's long-range Nimrod surveillance aircraft were relocated from RAF St, Mawgan, Cornwall, to Scotland the co-ordination centre was re-located north of the border too.   Without a role, RAF Mount Batten closed in 1992.

The RAF MARINE BRANCH

Many hold the mistaken belief that the RAF Marine Branch was an invention of the Second World War but in fact it is one of their oldest branches having been formed on 1st April 1918, the same day that the Royal Air Force itself came into existence. This was the day the Royal Flying Corps and the Royal Navy Air Service combined into one service, the Royal Air Force. However, at that time the Royal Navy also operated seaplanes and required marine craft to service them when at anchor. Transferred into the new Service, it was these craft which formed the basis of the RAF's first Marine Branch.

The expansion of the RAF's operations around the world from the 1920's onwards, invariably using flying boats as transport, also saw the growing need for marine craft and soon these were being operated in such diverse locations as Iceland to India or Nassau to Hong Kong. However it was from 1940 onwards that the Marine Branch really came into its own as the air war intensified.

For all aircrew operating over occupied Europe their last stage home involved crossing the waters of the English Channel. Many damaged aircraft failed to make the crossing, their crews either ditching on the water or bailing-out before the inevitable crash. Aircraft could be easily replaced from production lines but aircrew could not, manpower was short and the training of pilots and navigators a long process.

The RAF Marine Branch was the Service's answer to this problem, namely the speedy recovery of aircrew forced to land in the Channel. High speed rescue launches were soon deployed at strategic positions around Britain's coastline, including Exmouth and Plymouth.

As mentioned earlier, as the war progressed the importance of RAF Exeter grew as the 'first touchdown' for many stricken crews. However, for those who didn't make it the rescue launches at Exmouth were always on hand. This was the home of No.38 Air Sea Rescue Unit which first moved to the town in 1942 and stayed until just before 'D' day in 1944 when the vessels were moved to No.43 ASRU at RAF Mount Batten, Plymouth.

Surprisingly, there was no standardised design for the RAF's launches. They came in a wide variety of guises and were built in various boatyards throughout Southern England. These included the British Power Boat Company, Vospers and Thornycroft. Giving details of those early days was Leslie Pym, a former RAF marine engine fitter who served with the branch for most of the war and now lives in retirement at Exmouth. He recalls how when No.38 ASRU were first deployed at Exmouth they were equipped with two pinnaces., the serial number of one of these being 1247.

"These were general purpose craft whose role was to service seaplanes," he said. *"Whilst they were ideal for the job for which they were intended, they were quite slow and completely unsuitable for rescue operations where speed was of the essence. Fortunately this problem was solved with the building of High Speed Launches (HSL's) and as they became available the pinnaces at Exmouth were subsequently replaced by two of these faster vessels. These were built by John Thornycroft and given the serial nos. 191 and 193."*

For the statistically minded the Exmouth HSL's were 67 feet in length, with a beam of 15 feet and capable of a speed of 25 knots (approx. 30 mph). Les was asked about the power plants used in these vessels and he replied, *"The Exmouth launches were powered by two of Thornycroft's own petrol engines which were exceptionally noisy and it was once said they woke half the town up when started! However, generally speaking, most later craft were powered by what were originally aircraft engines, although contrary to some stories that got around at the time, they were not Merlins. Whilst the Merlin would have been ideal, they were needed desperately for aircraft and our needs were far down the chain. The most common power plant used in the later HSL's was the 500hp Napier Sea-Lion petrol engine. Each launch had three of these, giving a total output of 1500hp."*

The normal crew of each launch was nine and this comprised the Skipper (always an officer), the Coxswain (always a W.O or sergeant), Second Coxswain (a corporal), wireless operator, two fitters, a medical orderly and two other hands. However Les sometimes wondered how the selection process worked. *"I once came across a wireless operator who was complaining bitterly he'd been posted to the Marine Branch and he couldn't swim, "* said Les. *"Actually I think that was an exception as we all had swimming tests including one with all our kit on."*

Protection for the HSL's and their crew was provided by three small gun turrets. However the armament varied, initially being a single .303 Vickers machine gun which were later replaced by twin .303 Brownings. In some vessels of similar type the rear turret was replaced by a 20mm Oerlikon although this was not the case in respect of the Exmouth launches.

When the unit first moved to Exmouth the crews were billeted with local families who lived in the docks area of the town although later they were moved to the former Berkeley Hotel which was situated at the eastern end of Morton Crescent. However, whilst 'on call' the duty crew would stay in a wooden green bungalow at the dock entrance opposite the Starcross ferry steps. Aptly named 'Waterside', it was used as their HQ.

The launches themselves, particularly the duty one, were moored in the harbour entrance so they could quickly make open water if, and when, any emergency arose. To have moored within the harbour itself would have meant cranking the swing bridge open every time they put to sea!. However mooring in the entrance was not without its dangers and one former crewman recalls how one of the early pinnaces was jammed in the dock by a dredger whilst another recalls a later incident when HSL 193 was squeezed against the dock wall. This occurred whilst a small coaster was being negotiated through the entrance without the launch being moved to provide more room. The damage on that occasion was sufficient for 193 to be taken to the Morgan Giles Shipyard at Teignmouth for urgent repair.

Above: A 1942 photograph showing HSL 193 one of Exmouth's two
high speed launches built by Thornycroft. The other was 191.

Whilst the primary role of the Exmouth launches was to provide support for aircraft making strikes on targets across the Channel, interestingly this did not necessarily mean a dash from Exmouth when an emergency arose. When it was known a major operation was to take place the launches would be deployed to a much more appropriate rendezvous point in the Channel. For the Exmouth based craft this was known as RV 'B' which was approximately twenty-five miles south east of the town. However, waiting at the rendezvous point was not without some anxious moments for the crew as one member later recounted.

"It was situated in the middle of a mine field and nothing is a better laxative than having the engines switched off and being bounced around for hours at a time in a rough sea. We had to be bonkers!," he said.

Apart from mines, the vulnerability of the craft and its crew were also highlighted by another incident, now described.

"We were once used as target practice by a couple of Typhoons which were based at RAF Exeter and were using camera guns. We were later invited to the airfield to see the results, particularly of our evasive actions. They were frightening and I came to the conclusion that if attacked we really didn't stand much of a chance!"

During the two years the Marine Unit operated from Exmouth they were involved in a variety of rescues, not all with a happy ending. One concerned the rescue of a Spitfire pilot in July 1943. He'd parachuted into the sea off Dawlish and although the rescue had been effective the pilot dropped dead from shock when they got him onto the deck. However it wasn't only British airmen they were prepared to save. On another occasion they recovered the body of a dead German airman who was found to be wearing a thin leather strap around his neck which had two small onyx buttons attached. This discovery caused some interest because, apparently, it was the first time a larynx microphone had been seen in this country.

Visitors to Exmouth today may still see the rusting remains of a vessel stuck on the sands in the Exe estuary near Cockwood. The story behind the wreck is a Christmas tale with a difference. It was Christmas Day 1943 and the duty crew were just about to have their festive meal when they were scrambled to help a Dutch coaster which had been attacked by German E-boats and set on fire off Start Point. The launch assisted in towing the vessel to Exmouth where it was found to be un-seaworthy. Subsequently it was beached in the estuary where part of it still remains to this day.

As indicated earlier, the two Exmouth based HSL's Nos. 191 and 193, were transferred to RAF Mount Batten shortly before D-day where they continued to provide valuable support during the invasion period.

The role of Mount Batten as a Marine Branch base, amongst other operational duties, has already been mentioned in an earlier section and, with the end of WWII, its maritime duties were adapted to meet the requirements of the post-war era. Amongst these was the requirement for vessels able to undertake target-towing duties in addition to any rescue role.

Typical of these later vessels was Rescue & Target Towing Launch (RTTL) No.2757 which was designed by Vosper Ltd. of Portsmouth in 1956 and entered service with the RAF two years later. This vessel was much more powerful and faster than earlier models and was powered by two Rolls Royce Sea Griffon Mk.101 engines each producing 1700 hp which gave a top speed of 39 knots (approx 45 mph) and a cruising range of 530 nautical miles at 33 knots. It carried 2220 gallons with a consumption rate of 95 gallons per engine per hour at 2400 rpm. The vessel was also slightly larger than earlier models, with a length of 68 feet and a beam of 19 feet. The crew complement remained at nine.

RTTL MkII No. 2757

RTTL 2757, pictured above, served with No.1100 MCU, Alness, from 1958 to 1965 when, in the August, she was transferred to Mount Batten where she remained until June 1966. She was then transferred once again, this time to the MCU at Portrush where she served until the unit was closed in 1971. She then returned to Plymouth where she remained until decommissioned in November 1977 . However that is not the end of her story.

On the 26th November 1977, '2757' sailed from Plymouth and, after a sea voyage of 23 hours 40 minutes arrived at the Royal Victoria Docks in London. From here she undertook the last stage of her journey by road, to the superb RAF Museum at Hendon. Here she became a fitting and permanent reminder of the important role played by the RAF Marine Branch.

Another Plymouth based launch was Her Majesty's Air Force Vessel (HMAFV) 'Sea Otter' which had the service No.5002. Like RTTL 2757 she was a peace-time vessel and, unlike her wartime predecessors, carried no armament.

HMAFV 'Sea Otter' at RAF Mount Batten.

The vital role played by the RAF's Marine Units has often been under-estimated and, sadly, become largely forgotten in the years since its excellent small craft were taken out of service. However, the facts speak for themselves for it has been estimated that by the end of the war the RAF had operated over six hundred rescue craft from bases around the world and these had been instrumental in rescuing over 13,000 persons of whom well over half were skilled aircrew. The crews who served so well certainly lived up to their motto .

'The Sea Shall Not Have Them'.

The ROLE OF DEVON HOTELS

The influx of volunteers to join the RAF as aircrew was at times overwhelming which is just as well for Bomber Command casualties alone exceeded over 55,000 . However a high number of recruits also provided a major problem. Operational airfields were, as their name suggests, completely unsuitable for recruit training as, too, were the Flying Training Schools. Put simply, the RAF did not have the capacity to train high numbers of new recruits. There was also another problem. Existing RAF bases were potential enemy targets and indeed many sustained serious damage and suffered human casualties from Luftwaffe attacks. One solution was to requisition accommodation suitable for initial training which, in practice, meant large hotels situated in resort areas. As a result the initial postings for trainee aircrew was normally to an inland resort or one of the many coastal ones. Here hotels at Torquay, Paignton and Sidmouth were to make a major contribution to the war effort.

Soon many local hotels were providing accommodation and facilities for the first stage of aircrew training. Known as 'Initial Training Wings' (ITW), each was allocated an identifying number e.g. No. 2 ITW Torquay. Recruits would undergo parade ground drill, known in the services as 'square bashing', whilst at the same time embarking on a programme of physical fitness and basic classroom instruction in a variety of subjects.

Hotels were also commandeered for other purposes and mention has already been made of how naval aircrew operating from Haldon were billeted in a Teignmouth Hotel and similar accommodation was found for the RAF Marine Unit at Exmouth. Besides the requirement for billeting and training there was also another pressing need.
It was anticipated that casualties amongst aircrew would be high and, with trained aircrew a valuable resource, every attempt should be made to ensure their return to fitness and flying duties as soon as possible. Normal RAF Hospitals would be unable

to cope with the influx so alternative solutions became a priority.   One was to transfer minor operations and the recuperation of patients to other locations. Here the **Palace Hotel** in Torquay made a major contribution, being requisitioned as a RAF hospital as early as October 1939. Its role was to provide post-operative recuperation for officer aircrew and also   surgical facilities within its in-house operating theatre. It is perhaps ironic that, designated as a military hospital, it was the only Torbay hotel to suffer substantial enemy damage. .

The Palace Hotel, Torquay.

The Palace Hotel before it was bombed in October 1942.

It is to the hotel's credit that over sixty years later they still have a record of those historic days which includes photographs of patients and staff, the devastation, press cuttings and testimonials from former aircrew. Many former aircrew, now living locally, have personal recollections of the **Palace,** and Torbay ITWs, and these appear in the following pages.

Cover of the Palace Hotel's Record Book

The **Palace** entered the annals of local history at around 1110 hours on the morning of Sunday, 25th October 1942, when a flight of four FW-190's took the town by surprise and administered a devastating blow. They flew back across the Channel leaving many dead and injured, particularly at the **Palace** where a direct hit had virtually demolished the east wing.

A newspaper dated the next day reported an account of the raid but, because of censorship, made no reference of the fact it was an RAF Hospital.

The newspaper report, no doubt through censorship, makes no reference of the fact it was an RAF Hospital.   The opening paragraphs read as follows:

'Flying low along the coast yesterday morning four FW190's swerved over a South-West seaside town, dropping bombs and firing cannon before turning out to sea again, but not at least before one of them was seen leaving a trail of smoke.   The leading plane dived to tree-top height to make a direct hit on a hospital.   It is feared that casualties amongst both men and women are high ...."

However the Palace archives and newspaper report are not the only source of information on that infamous day for Miss Kay Harte, a VAD serving there, also kept a diary and under her entry for that day she wrote:

"In the Theatre when we were bombed at 11.10 - one direct hit & one v. near miss - 19 killed, not all found - ghastly thing - rain fell all day - we evacuated patients. injured (40) to sick quarters at the Torbay and ours to Wroughton - just a few of the ill ones. It was an amazing thing - no panic. Little Tinker-Bell was killed also G/C Whittle. W/C Burke, Luddington and many others. - we, all the VAD's, were sent to a nursing home for the night."

Then entries for the following days continue with that for Monday, 26th October, beginning :

"Hectic day disposing of patients - sick leave or Wroughton for most of them. More bits of bodies found - awful. .... "

Speaking to Kay over sixty years after the event she still recalls the finer details. She was serving as a VAD (Voluntary Aid Detachment), which was a detachment of the Red Cross, and her main role was that of the Clinical Orthopaedic Secretary. This not only entailed keeping all the patients' records but also taking notes in the operating theatre during orthopaedic surgery and helping in other respects too.

She was in the Theatre when the bombs struck and had been assisting in 'dipping bandages' for the surgeon at the time In fact, to this day Kay maintains that being in the surgery probably saved her life. There was no warning before they heard the first bomb fall, landing just away from the building itself. Nevertheless the blast made the building shake to such an extent that it dislodged the light above the operating table. Then, only moments later, the second bomb hit and virtually demolished the hospital's east wing. Had she not been in the Theatre Kay would have been in her office and undoubtedly either killed or seriously injured by the blast.

61

25 SUNDAY (298-67)

21st after Trinity

Sun rises 6.40. Sun sets 4.48. Moon sets 7.44 a.m. Moon rises 5.53 p.m.

*In op. Theatre when we were bombed at 11.10 — one died but one
v. near miss — 19 killed, not all found — ghastly
thing — rain fell all day — we evacuated patients, injured
(40 to sick quarters & the Torbay & ones to Broughton
— just a few of the ill ones — It was an
amazing thing — no panic. Little Tinker Bell was
killed also G/c Whittle, W/c Burke, Luddington
& many others — we, all the V.A.Dr were sent to a
Nursing Home for the night.*

26 MONDAY (299-66)

*Hectic day disposing of patients — sick leave &
Broughton for most of them — More bits of
bodies found — awful. Keith phoned at
lunch time:
Out to dinner with John & Nic & Joan — all, or nearly
all V.A.Dr were sent off —
& visited patients in Torbay & S.S.Q with John
and Nic.*

27 TUESDAY (300-65)

*More clearing up — sent off all folder &
X rays to Broughton —
Dinner with John again after we
visited the patients.*

The relevant extract from Kay's diary.

She also stresses the fact that the casualties, later put at twenty killed and some forty injured, would have been much higher had it not been for the fact Dan Maskell, the Physiotherapist, had taken a lot of the RAF's 'battle casualties' away on a day's outing. In fact records show that at the time of the raid hospital was technically full with 203 in-patients. Once the dust settled an enormous task still lay ahead as Kay now explains:

"Our primary task was to evacuate all of our patients which we did with the utmost of speed and to continue treatment at their new hospitals. It was also necessary for their notes to follow them and that was my job. I spent the next six days in what can best be described as rubble without windows trying to sort all the records out. Fortunately most survived and were forwarded on as required and then I, too, said goodbye to The Palace."

One of the early patients to recuperate at the Palace was Spitfire pilot, Keith Lawrence. Keith, a New Zealander came to Britain in 1939 and, surviving the brunt of the Battle of Britain, was shot down shortly afterwards whilst engaged in combat with four enemy Me 109's, one of which shot the wing off his Spitfire. Luckily he managed to bale out over the Channel and was rescued. However serious leg injuries necessitated hospitalisation between November 1940 and November 1941, the latter part of which was spent at the Palace.

He recalls how he had met Kay whilst she was a VAD at an earlier hospital where he'd first been a patient and then how, with leg still heavily plastered, he was transferred for convalescence to the Palace. By sheer co-incidence they needed a new Clinical Orthopaedic Secretary and Kay found herself posted to Torquay at the same time as Keith's move. Keith was full of praise for the facilities and staff there but by the beginning of 1942 his recuperation was complete and he was posted into the thick of battle again. Leaving Kay behind he made the hazardous journey to Malta to become the C.O of a Spitfire Squadron at the height of the island's siege. It was here he was awarded the DFC.

There is a happy end to this story for, when war ended in 1945, Keith and Kay were married and today live in happy retirement in Exeter.

Kay and Keith, leg in plaster, at the Palace in 1941.

The raid of October 25th 1942 put the **Palace** out of commission for the rest of the war. It re-opened in March 1948. The following photographs show the extent of the damage. Note the gap in the first one.

The damage to the **Palace** is unique because it was a military hospital and, reportedly, was marked with a Red Cross. However the raid itself was not unusual for records show that the Torbay area was often a target for hit-and-run raiders. In fact post-war analysis of records show that it was a favourite target for Luftwaffe pilots of the 10 Staffel of JG2 who lived in style at the Chateau de Louvigny and flew from their base at Carpiquet on the outskirts of Caen. From there it was a mere 170 miles across the Channel to Torbay, little more than 1/2 hour flying time. It is known they were re-equipped with the FW 190 in the Summer of 1942.

The ground attack version of the FW190 similar to that used in the raid
on the Palace Hotel.   The bomb rack beneath the fuselage held a 500kg bomb.

Another patient at the Palace who makes mention of the raid was Norman Conquer,
who now lives at Okehampton and whose story is told later in the book.   The sole
survivor when his aircraft crashed, he spent eight months in hospital before being sent
to The Palace to convalesce as he now recalls.

*"What a splendid place to choose as an officers' convalescent home.   For most of
us our treatment began in the hotel gym immediately on arrival and we soon
discovered that physiotherapy at the Hotel was in the charge of Dan Maskell, of
tennis fame.   My room mate was a Canadian pilot who survived a crash but
suffered arm and neck injuries, his tall neck-brace making him look like a 'giraffe'
lady from Africa !   With my leg in a full length plaster we were an odd couple !
However despite our handicaps we soon discovered a bus stop only a hundred yards
from the hotel and most convenient for daily forays into town although,
unfortunately, my plaster wouldn't allow me the luxury of sitting down for the
journey.   Needless to say we enjoyed the hospitality of the local pubs !   Sadly
there were always events to highlight the fact we were still very much at war.*

A few days after I left to return to duty the Palace was bombed by FW 190 intruders and several of the inmates killed. One really never knew what might be in store."

The raid was also recalled by former pilot Frank Burdekin of Sidmouth who, on his nineteenth birthday, had reported to the Aircrew Reception Centre at the **Sefton Hotel,** Babbacombe, He recalls:

" The worst experience was being given all the 'jabs' in one go instead of over a period of days. I retired to bed on the third floor feeling the end was near when, shortly afterwards, there was an awful crash and the window fell out - 'hit and run' raiders had dropped bombs just down the road, on the Palace Hotel, killing a number of RAF officers convalescing there."

Today the Palace has risen from the ashes. Reopening in March 1948, and since greatly modernised, it is once more a fine hotel. However for many wounded RAF aircrew they will always have a soft spot for the 'hospital' which to them was always a 'hotel'.

Torbay's ITW's

Many other hotels were commandeered for the initial training of aircrew and designated as ACRC's (Aircrew Reception Centres) or ITWs (Initial Training Wings). Of all the towns in the UK where their requisition was at its highest, arguably Torbay's combination of Torquay and Paignton came close to topping the list. Another Sidmouth man who attended ACRC at the already mentioned **Sefton Hotel** was former bomber pilot John Morgan who continued his training at No.5 ITW in Torquay. Like so many others, for him it is memories of the comradeship and the pubs which linger strongest today.

He recalls his second day in the RAF at Babbacombe when he had been issued with only part of his uniform and had gone down the road dressed in RAF trousers, held up by standard issue white webbing belt, a civilian shirt and no hat.

Suddenly a large saloon car pulled up beside him and a young officer jumped out. "Why didn't you salute the flag ?", he demanded. "What flag?" asked John. The small pennant on the front of the car was pointed out to him and he was told that it denoted an Air Commodore was on board. With that the rear door opened an John was beckoned over by the very senior officer whom it transpired was doing an inspection tour of the area's training facilities. Answering his questions John explained it was only his second day and that was all the uniform he had. Upon this he was ordered to 'double back' to the hotel. "What does 'double' mean", John innocently asked. "It means run you bloody fool, run", came the terse reply.

John also relates another amusing episode which was part of their daily routine and involved the 'prim and proper' elderly ladies of Torbay. He explains:

"Part of our daily routine of physical exercise was a run down to the beach followed by a dip in the sea," he says. *" Whilst we were issued with swimming gear we weren't too fussy about how we changed and so at any one time there were usually quite a few nude airmen around. Whilst the young ladies of Torquay might have appreciated the spectacle the older ones did not . Letters of complaint frequently came in and although orders were issued to be more decorous I'm not that sure that we were."*

John's flying career came to an abrupt end on the 12th August 1941 when he was briefed for his first 'op', a raid on Berlin. He piloted his aircraft to within sight of the city when it was hit my enemy fire and burst into flames. With a full bomb load on

69

board he and his crew wasted no time in baling out. Injured in the process, he was taken prisoner of war. He was only nineteen.

However the **Sefton Hotel** was also used as No.1 ITW and one person who undertook his initial training there was Arthur McCartney who later became the Deputy Chief Constable of the former Devon Constabulary. He recounts:

" *My unit from ACRC arrived late in the year. We swam or paddled in the sea on Christmas Day 1941. We were housed in the **Sefton Hotel** on Babbacombe Cliff Road and ate in an hotel, the name of which I have been unable to recall and which was in the Cary Park district. The course consisted of drill, PT, lectures, sport and medical checks. At the top of the road through the Village was the Babbacombe Garage and we were instructed in navigation in its basement. Our course was completed early in 1942 and I remember how we formed up and marched from the **Sefton Hotel** to Torre Railway Station. To me it was reminiscent of films I had seen at the cinema with troops marching off to war in the Great War. We sang 'It's a Long Way to Tipperary' and 'Roll me Over' and such but we were only going to the Elementary Navigation School in Eastbourne !!"*

Then he added, " *I also remember a very attractive young lady who worked in a cake shop along the main road. She was certainly an asset to the owner, we were always popping in there for cakes and buns! I'm sure eventually she must have married someone who became aircrew and I often wonder what happened to her. So many husbands were killed , I hope she was lucky."*

Arthur went on to become one of Bomber Command's most experienced Bomb Aimers. Flying well into his second tour of operations, he participated in thirteen of the sixteen major raids on Berlin and is thought to be the only 'Air Bomber' to be twice awarded the DFC.   By co-incidence another former senior officer of the local Constabulary also undertook basic training in Torquay. He was Alf Wallen, whose story appears later in the book but recalls those early days here:

*"I was at No. 13 ITW which was based in Torquay's **Grand Hotel.** Our course director was Flying Officer Tom Goddard, an excellent cricketer who played for Gloucestershire and was an England spin bowler. Most mornings it was PT behind Torquay railway station followed by marching up and down Torquay sea front at 140 paces a minute. Nearly all our course work was done in the **Grand Hotel** but occasionally we would parade on the Green about three hundred yards from the **Grand** and take down Morse code messages sent by Aldis Lamp from a bedroom at the **Belgrave Hotel.***

Jack Atkinson of Sampford Peverell, who went on to fly the Hurricane, Tomahawk and Mustang, recalls his initial training at No. 2 ITW between April and June 1941 although he says much of the experience is a now a blur.

*"I was stationed in a small hotel on the Harbour front which I believe was called **'The Beacon'.** I remember the PTI's (Physical Training Instructors) marching our entry up and down by the harbour and also there was a running track on Daddy Hole Plain which is also where we were given Aldis lamp instruction. However I suppose my main recollection is of the pubs and an early visit one morning by a Heinkel 111 which caused us some consternation when it opened machine gun fire before dropping its bombs nearby. Thankfully, none of us was hurt but it was a close call. Its funny to look back now but a few months later we were doing the same thing.*

Photographs of recruits in those early days are comparatively rare. The one on the left is of Jack Atkinson, on the left, during on off-duty momernt on The Strand, Torquay, in 1941.

Below is Daddyhole Plain as it is today but over sixty years ago it was a PT ground and running track for trainee aircrew.

Another Torbay seafront hotel which was commandeered by the RAF was The *Tembani* at Paignton although it has since been converted.   John Legg of Budleigh Salterton recalls being there between the 24th August and 11th October 1940 and how they were marched everywhere singing such songs as 'I've got sixpence' and 'Nellie Dean' as they went, renderings which he says were much appreciated by the locals ! He says they could not afford much 'night-life' on two shillings (20p) a day.

One interesting moment he recalls was being marched to the grassy area above the Babbacombe Cliff to be addressed by the 'Father of the RAF' Lord Trenchard who always carried a walking stick.   However, his talk was interrupted by an air-raid warning just as a German Ju-88 flew overhead from inland and headed out to sea with Lord Trenchard waving his stick .   On another occasion John was on guard duty when, early in the morning, the corporal in charge came out and gave him five rounds of .303 ammunition, announcing there was believed to be an invasion further down the coast to the West.   He says he never did find out what led to the scare.

Pictured left is John Legg as part of a group photograph taken in Torbay during the Summer of 1940. John became a successful Coastal Command pilot striking at enemy shipping and completed a tour on Hudsons.

Founder of the East Devon Branch of the ACA and now its vice-president, Don Francis recalls his ITW days at yet another Torquay hotel, **The Templestowe** situated in Tor

Church Road. He had been working in the aircraft industry since leaving school and joined the Royal Auxiliary Air Force as an aero-engine fitter in 1937, volunteering for full-time service in February 1939. When war was declared he was restricted from volunteering for aircrew but when the opportunity arose in the summer of 1942 he wasted no time in doing so and was selected for navigator training.

The Templestowe Hotel in 2005.

Don says,   *"I arrived at the Templestowe in August 1942 as an LAC (Leading Aircraftsman) with one   Good Conduct Badge.   Being a visible indication of service - three years of undetected crime - it worried the newly appointed corporal PTI's who expected me to be an 'awkward type'.   However, the threat, constant through aircrew training, of being failed ' LMF' (Lack of Moral Fibre) kept my awkwardness under control.   I even helped one of the junior officers by giving talks on Air Force Law and procedure !   I was also put in charge of the squad and responsible for marching them to lectures.   P.T was a regular feature.   This mostly comprised of a run to Cockington where we took refreshment, at our own expense, in the Drum Inn where, incidentally, the NCO in charge of us always seemed to have a 'freebe'.   Then we would hang around until it was time to return, a journey which would usually find us running into the sea dressed in our shorts and singlets. Dinghy drill was a not to be forgotten experience with us lining up to jump off the harbour wall into the sea which, when the tide was out this could be a drop of up to fourteen feet.   Then we would swim to a one-man dinghy into which we would climb with difficulty"*

Don qualified as a navigator and went on to fly thirty-five ops with a 'special duties' Mosquito squadron engaged on low level intruder missions. After the war he returned to the aviation business and became De Havilland's Chief Draughtsman for their 'Blue Streak' missile project, before joining British Aerospace from which he retired in 1981. He is still a Member of the Royal Aeronautical Society.

Other Torbay hotels used for the initial training of aircrew included The **Palm Court,** the home of No.5 ITW, and also the **Foxlands.** The Torbay area continued to attract RAF recruits even when the war was reaching its closing stages as Bill Nicholson of Exeter recalls:

*" I arrived in October 1944 and was taken to the '**Foxlands Hotel'** which acted as the unit's HQ.   Here we came across our first demand for 'name and last three' - last three what ?!.   The clerk in charge took great delight in explaining to us morons that 'last three' meant the last three digits of our service number.   The system worked well most of the time , except later when I started getting back*

somebody else's laundry - a chap with similar name but whose number differed from mine in one digit. Another surprise, for me at least, was that we would be scattered around the town in various hotels. I'd assumed we'd all be in one barrack block.

*Our first billet as in **Alta Vista**, a guest house or small hotel in Windsor Road. Down its drive and across the road were two small hotels (names forgotten), one was the cook-house and mess hall and the other given over to lecture rooms. In mid-November we moved into **The Devonshire**, a large hotel, very good with excellent food. I heard that the head chef had stayed on after the hotel had been commandeered."*

The Special Role of Sidmouth Hotels.

At Sidmouth a number of hotels helped play a different role. Sid Pitt, now sadly deceased, once recalled how an 'Officer's Training School' was set up in the town between 1942-43 and drew its students from aircrew officers who had undertaken their flying training abroad but had yet to join an operational squadron.

Sid, who retired to Honiton, had been a weapons instructor at the 'School' and instrumental in preparing a 'Battle Training Ground' on Mutters Moor. This tract of open moor with its growth of heather and gorse lies high above the town on the road to Otterton and provided an ideal location for the construction of a 'commando' style assault course and a grenade range. Sid said that the emphasis had been on fitness training utilising the newly installed assault course. However the grenade range also served a wider purpose, being additionally used for instruction in the use of small arms and explosives. Camouflage techniques were also taught, an essential subject bearing in mind the object of the course was to teach how to evade capture if shot down in hostile territory.   Later Sid, an expert marksman, was to fly on 'ops' as a waist gunner on a B-17 Flying Fortress.

Today visitors to the town do not realise that the car park near the **Bedford Hotel** was once a drill square whilst aircrew were stationed in the hotel itself along with other hotels such as the **Knole, Belmont** and **Fortfield.**   The officers' mess was in the **Riviera Hotel** and that for Sergeants in the **Torbay.**   Sidmouth's **Victoria Hotel** housed the medical section.

Very little vestiges of the assault course or grenade range remain on Mutters Moor but one reminder of those days has been preserved on the cliff top at the entrance to Connaught Gardens, only a few minutes walk from the Victoria Hotel and on the way to Mutters Moor. This is the gun emplacement illustrated in the above photograph.   It is now embellished with a 'Blue Plaque' signifying it as part of the town's heritage.

The Nuffield Scheme.

Don Francis, who attended ITW at the **Templestowe** during 1942, also returned to the resort later during the war and whilst taking a well-earned break from flying operations. His return, he says, was thanks to a scheme which is largely forgotten today.

Here he explains:

*"This was a scheme financed by Lord Nuffield under which all operational aircrew were given   10/-   (£0.50p) a day spending money whilst on a week's leave from operational flying.   However, as an alternative to the ten shillings you could elect to stay in a good hotel for a week.   One of the hotels participating in this scheme was **The Imperial** in Torquay and I opted to take my week's leave there, accompanied by my wife.   I have many happy memories of that week during which the hotel treated us as VIPs.*

My stay was free and I paid £5.5s for my wife. I kept the bill for years but it is now in The AirCrew Association's archives."

Footnote: Only a brief mention has been made of the service history of a number of aircrew, such as Arthur McCartney, whose recollections of Torbay hotels are recorded within this book. This is because their full stories have been covered in earlier volumes, namely *'Touchdown East Devon'* or *'East Devon Aircrew & Airfields'*.

A number   of the hotels mentioned in this chapter no longer exist.   Some have changed their use whilst others, such as the Foxlands, have been bulldozed to the ground to make way for housing development.

The RAF and ALLIED AIR FORCES MEMORIAL

Standing on Plymouth Hoe is the RAF and Allied Air Forces Memorial which, since 1945, is known to be the only one to have been built that acknowledges the indebtedness owed to every man and woman of the British Isles, the Commonwealth, and those from many other countries who served in all Commands of the Royal Air Force and Allied Air Forces. It especially records our gratitude to the United States of America for the major part played by that country in the air war, particularly over Europe, the substantial losses sustained by them and those of our other main Ally, the USSR.

The monument, erected in 1989, depicts the bronze figure of an 'Unknown Airman' fully kitted in a flying suit and wearing his Mae West life-jacket. In his right hand he is carrying his parachute pack in readiness for the flight ahead. The grey marble column below is enhanced by a black marble inlay listing the many countries whose aircrew are commemorated here together with various tributes to the role they played. It also lists the losses of the three main Air Forces engaged in the conflict:

107,000 Members of the Royal Air Force.
84,000 Members of the United States Air Force.
43,200 Members of the Soviet Air Force.
who made the ultimate sacrifice.
They flew by Day and Night
and gave their lives to keep forever Bright
That precious light
Freedom

The ashes of the late Air Vice Marshal Don Bennett, CB, CBE, DSO, have since been interred at the base of the plinth, a fitting resting place for a great airman whose foresight led to the formation of the elite 'Path Finder Force' which spearheaded so many of the Allied raids on occupied Europe and the Nazi homeland.

As a result of numerous requests, and the formation of a Committee by the Plymouth Branch of The AirCrew Association on which all RAF organisations are represented, an annual service of dedication now takes place at the memorial on the morning of the last Sunday in June. Many come to pay tribute, including representatives from foreign Embassies, civic leaders, veterans, families and friends of those in whose honour the memorial stands.

Personal Recollections

of

Those who Served

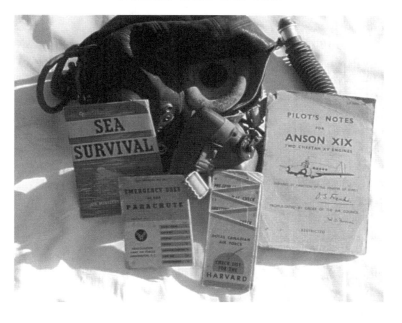

' When once you have tasted flight, you will forever walk
the earth with your eyes turned skyward, for there you
have been, and there you will always long to return'

Leonardo da Vinci   1452-1519

Our thanks go to the following members of the AirCrew Association for contributing their personal stories to this book.

BLAIR, David.	Pilot.
BOWER, Tony.	Pilot.
CONQUER, Norman OBE.	Pilot.
COOK, Kenneth DFC.	Navigator.
DABIN, Victor.	Pilot.
DANCKWARDT, Frederick.	Air Gunner.
DODD, Ray.	Air Electronics Officer.
DURRANT, John MBE.	Pilot.
FORBES, Ian.	Pilot.
GERMAN, John.	Pilot.
GRIFFITH, Harold.	Pilot.
GROOCOCK, Deryck. AFC.	Pilot.
HEAL, Adrian.	Wireless Operator.
HURRELL, Stanley.	Bomb Aimer.
JENKINS, Michael.	Pilot.
JOHNSON, Samuel.	Wireless Operator/Air Gunner.
OAKEY, Trevor AFC.	Pilot.
POLLITT, Kenneth.	Flight Engineer.
PRICE, John.	Navigator.
REVILL, Harold.	Pilot.
ROGERS, Gerald.	Wireless Operator/ Air Gunner.
SIMKINS, Stacey.	Wireless Operator/ Air Gunner.
SMITH, Cyril MBE.	Observer.
WALLEN, Alfred MBE.	Navigator.
WALTER, Norman.	Air Gunner.
WARREN, John.	Pilot.
WOOTTON, George.	Air Gunner.
WRIGHT, Clifford DFM.	Navigator.
YOUNG, Frank AEA.	Pilot.

ACTION in the FAR EAST.

David BLAIR

David Blair was born in Dunfermline, Scotland, in October 1922 and joined the RAF shortly before his nineteenth birthday. Volunteering for aircrew, he was assessed suitable for training as a pilot and after ITW at Scarborough was posted to No.34 EFTS Assimiboia in Canada. Here he commenced basic flying training on the Tiger Moth before progressing to more advanced flying on Harvards at No.39 SFTS at Swift Current and No.37 SFTS, Calgary. Awarded his pilot's wings, David returned to the UK for the last stage of his training at No.58 OTU at Grangemouth, Scotland, where he flew the Spitfire.

His first operational posting was to No.110 (H) Squadron based in the Far East at Khumbirgram in Assam where he found himself flying the Vultee Vengeance dive-bomber against Japanese military targets. As the offensive proved successful and there was a gradual retreat of Japanese forces, the Squadron was moved to India to re-equip with the Mosquito. However, meanwhile, a detachment from the Squadron was sent to Takoradi on the Gold Coast to carry out experimental DDT spraying. David's return to the Far East did not materialise for he was posted to European operations and No.183 Squadron which was operating Typhoons against enemy targets in

Holland and Germany. Asked about memorable wartime incidents it was one of these strikes which he recalls.

" I was operating from a PSP strip at Nijmagen on the morning 'Operation Varsity' commenced, perhaps better known as the 'Rhine Crossing', when my Squadron was briefed to suppress German flak sites to the east of the Rhine and west of the autobahn between Wesel and Bocholt. Our Typhoons each carried two 1,000lb cases containing sixty-four barometrically fused anti-personnel bombs and during my first attack my bombs failed to release and I was left with both on open hooks. Trying to release them with rapid deceleration and accompanying cannon firing failed to do the trick and left me with no option but to return to the strip and land. However, on touch-down both cases shot off their carriers and burst open, scattering sixty-four bombs around the threshold. Fortunately none exploded and the awaiting armourers were able to collect them in time to allow the other aircraft to land. Nevertheless it was a near thing and gave me quite a fright !"

Post war David decided to remain in the RAF and spent four years between 1946 and 1950, as an instructor in Flying Training Command where he taught trainee pilots to fly a variety of aircraft from Tiger Moths to Harvards. It was whilst an instructor in 1948 he was granted a permanent commission.

By 1950 the RAF was already into the early jet age and the Cold War provided a threat to the Western World. David returned to squadron service with a posting to No.2 Allied Tactical Air Force (ATAF) in Germany where he flew the RAF's first jet fighters, the Vampire and Meteor, with Nos.4 and 112 Squadrons. However, this was also a period of enhanced technical design of fighter aircraft and the US built Sabre was one of the new breed which had proved its worth in air battles over Korea. It was time to re-equip squadrons in Europe and in 1953 David was transferred to No.147

Squadron, Transport Command, with the task of ferrying Sabres across the Atlantic for re-deployment with squadrons based in the UK and Germany.

When this role ended David entered a phase in his career which was to see him undertaking a number of interesting and varied tasks over a period of some twelve years. These began in 1954 when he was assigned for two years to HQ No.17 Group Fighter Command as Weapons Officer. It was also a period when more types of aircraft were being added to his log book. These included the Anson, Oxford, Hunter, Venom and the RAF's then new trainer, the Chipmunk.

Another flying posting followed, this time to the Central Fighter Establishment at West Raynham in Norfolk where he joined their Air Fighting Development Squadron and saw a further three aircraft types added to his log book, namely the Supermarine Swift, Jet Provost and the Folland Gnat. Then, in 1958, David went North of the border to RAF Leuchars, Scotland, for a three year appointment as the Wing Operations Officer following which he moved South to RAF Linton-on-Ouse in North Yorkshire. Here he became the Station Test Pilot, a role which entailed testing the air-worthiness of all the station's aircraft which had undergone recent major maintenance or repair.

However, arguably some would say that his most interesting post-war tour came in 1962 when he was seconded to the British Antarctic Survey. Operating from a base on Adelaide Island, he spent almost two years flying a De Havilland Otter, equipped with wheel / ski landing gear, in sub-zero temperatures over the icy wastes of the Antarctic. Their role was to support the geologists and surveyors lay depots and re-supply the bases, a task which involved conveying personnel and dog teams. The two aircraft were wintered on Deception Island for hangar and maintenance facilities .

When the secondment ended in 1964 David returned to RAF Leuchars where he was appointed Flying Wing Adjutant. However the following year and now a Flt.Lt. with 24 years service, he realised the chances of another flying tour were diminishing and somewhat reluctantly he decided to take retirement so he could continue his love of flying in a civilian capacity.

In 1966 he joined 'Airwork Service Training' as a flying instructor at their civilian flying school at Scone in Scotland, later becoming the Flight Manager of their Instrument Training Flight. He was to remain with them for fourteen years when another flying opportunity presented itself. This was with 'Ashbon Aviation Ltd' which was based at King Khalid Military City in Saudi Arabia. However if David's photograph looks familiar to local aviation enthusiasts this is because on his return to the UK in 1983 he spent the next ten years as a flying instructor with the Exeter Flying Club and Airways Flight Training.

He finally closed the last of his many flying log books in 1993, books which had recorded over half a century of aviation history from wartime operations against both the Japanese and the Germans, to service in the Middle East and helping civilian novices to fly. By the time of his journey's end he had flown thirty-five different types of aircraft and amassed the remarkable total of 14,580 flying hours, truly a master pilot !

Today David and his wife, Peggy, enjoy a peaceful retirement in the Preston area of Paignton and he continues to enjoy the company of fellow aviators as a member of the Torbay branch of The AirCrew Association.

Two training aircraft widely used for the training of pilots during WWII.

Top: The de Havilland Tiger Moth used as an elementary trainer, mainly at EFTS's in the UK and Rhodesia.   Bottom: The North American Harvard used as a standard and advanced trainer throughout the UK, Canada and Rhodesia. The one shown was flown by No.1 FTS, RCAF Centralia, Ontario.

WHIRLYBIRDS to the RESCUE in ANTARCTICA

Tony BOWER

Tony Bower was born near Leeds in May 1942 and educated at Shrewsbury School. On finishing his education he initially opted for a career in insurance but at the age of 21 decided to seek some excitement in the Royal Navy before settling down. Selected for training as a pilot, Tony's first stage of training was carried out at HMS Britannia, the Royal Naval College at Dartmouth. *"It was an interesting time "*, he said, *"for not only were we learning the rudiments of naval life but they were also trying to make officers of us. Additionally, for those of us who were going on to fly, there was the added excitement of flying in what must have been one of the last Tiger Moths in military service and was based at Roborough."*

Leaving Dartmouth, the next stage of Tony's training was basic fixed-wing flying on the RAF's primary trainer, the Chipmunk, at the RAF Flying Training School, Linton-on-Ouse. However he had been chosen to fly helicopters and, after successfully completing his fixed-wing training, he was appointed to RNAS Culdrose, Helston, where initial helicopter training was undertaken on the Hiller 12E and Whirlwind Mks 3 & 7.

Advanced training was carried during late 1964 and early 1965, initially at RNAS Culdrose and later at HMS Osprey, the RNAS base at Portland where Tony flew the Wessex MkI. Still flying the Wessex, his first squadron appointment came through later in 1965 when he joined 820 Squadron aboard the aircraft carrier HMS Eagle. In addition to its complement of Wessex helicopters, it was also equipped with Buccaneer, Gannet and Sea Vixen aircraft together with three Scimitars for re-fuelling purposes.

Explaining the helicopter role, Tony said *"Basically our Wessex provided all-weather anti-submarine patrols. Equipped with sonar domes which we would lower into the water, our all-weather plus night-flying capability actually put us ahead of the Americans at that time. Another of our duties was to act as 'Plane Guard', in other words to rescue any fixed-wing crews who may have ditched.*

Another unexpected role came whilst we were in Singapore. The future of the Fleet Air Arm was looking uncertain as the Wilson government had recently axed the carrier fleet. Then, out of the blue, we were ordered to patrol the Beira Strait off East Africa. We quickly left Singapore and crossed the Indian Ocean unobserved to arrive off the east coast of Africa. Ian Smith had declared UDI in Southern Rhodesia and we had been sent to enforce the ensuing blockade. The result was that we were at sea for a continuous period of eighty-two days, then a peace-time record. Interestingly the BBC made a superb documentary about life on board the Eagle at that time which provided very good scenes on board with an interesting left-wing political stance."

On completion of his ship's tour Tony returned to RNAS Culdrose to await his next appointment which was to see him sailing South to the Antarctic. This was a two year tour undertaken between 1967-1969, flying the helicopters based on ships covering the Antarctic surveys. The first was the Royal Navy's hydrographic survey vessel, HMS Protector, which at that time was the oldest ship in the navy and not ice-strengthened. It was equipped with the Whirlwind Mk9 and he later flew the same type when transferred to HMS Endurance which was strengthened to go through thick ice. Under the Antarctic Treaty the ships could be used for scientific purposes only. It was a period with many memories some of which he now relates.

"Obviously in a climate like that there were always a few anxious moments but none like that of the RAF crew we rescued ! A Squadron Leader, flying with his Sergeant co-pilot, was assisting the British Antarctic Survey Expedition and had been flying their Twin Otter over a snow covered mountainous area when they became lost and low on fuel. Miraculously they managed to land on an ice shelf having descended, uncertain of their position, through cloud. A distress call was made but, unfortunately for them, the weather was atrocious and, with very little visibility, it took us five days before we were able to cross a 5000 feet high mountain range. Luckily they were still in pretty good shape and the aircraft was undamaged. We managed to fly in under low cloud with a load of fuel in 40 gallon drums which we quickly pumped into the tanks of the Twin Otter. Then, with the weather worsening by the minute, we quickly departed and the Twin Otter took off shortly afterwards. They obviously made their base safely for I later heard that the Squadron Leader's next appointment was as the CO of the RAF Survival School!

Another aspect of this tour was our association with the Falklands and also with the Argentine bearing in mind this was some years before the conflict. One of our tasks was to survey the channel up to Chartres so that the supply ship, Darwin, could safely navigate it. On another occasion we picked up Lord Chalfont in Montevideo and took him to the Falkland Islands where we then flew him to meet the local people on the settlements. They made it very clear to him by flying many Union Jacks that they were totally opposed to the Labour Government's plans to hand them over to the Argentine."

The above photograph is of one of HMS Endurance's aircraft on Antarctic ice whilst the header photograph is of Tony taken around this period.

He continues, *"Of course, at that time relations between Argentina and Britain were pretty normal and although there were restrictions on our entering their ports direct from the Falklands we could do so if our last port was elsewhere. It was on such an occasion that we sailed with Endurance into Puerto Belgrano having previously left Montevideo in Uruguay. In true aircrew fellowship, the other ship's pilot, observers and myself, were invited to a nearby air base where we were given a tour and left very impressed by their professionalism. It was no surprise to us, when the conflict came, that they were highly effective, unlike the Argentine army. Later during that visit we made friends with their padre at a cocktail party, He was proud of his Irish descent although he'd never been there and we were invited to have dinner with him a couple of nights later. It was a very enjoyable occasion and as we were leaving he presented us with a bottle of wine. It was only when we arrived back on ship that we discovered it was communion wine !*

On return to the UK, and after a brief leave, I sailed with HMS Endurance to the Arctic to pick up Wally Herbert and his team of three who had sledged with dogs from Alaska via the North Pole to the north of Spitzbergen. The ice was breaking up and the 'pick-up' was in fact more of a rescue ! The magnetic field certainly built in quite large errors on the aircraft's compass but fortunately the ship's radar was in good order as the visibility was not too good. Interestingly, within a few weeks I'd crossed both the Antarctic and Arctic Circle lines of latitude."

The Whirlwind

His duties with Endurance completed, Tony once more teamed up with the RAF, this time at RAF Turnhill where he passed out as a Qualified Helicopter Instructor. This qualification saw him appointed to the Royal Navy's 706 Squadron where for the next two years he trained naval pilots on Wessex and Wasp helicopters.

In 1971 he opted to leave the Royal Navy at the eight-year point of his engagement, returning to the world of finance as a Financial Advisor. In 1977 he and his wife Frances moved to Budleigh Salterton since when he's enjoyed his hobbies of sailing, golf and croquet.

SOLE SURVIVOR !

Norman P.W. CONQUER, OBE

Norman Conquer was born in Tottenham in February 1921 and educated at Tottenham Grammar School and Royal Liberty School, Romford, before starting work with a company of insurance brokers in the City. Aged eighteen when war was declared, Norman immediately volunteered for aircrew duties and was accepted into the RAF in December, 1939.

However, not everything went according to plan. Whilst accepted as potential aircrew, at the recruiting office he was given the choice of 'immediate service' or to 'go home and await the call for training.' *"Naively,"* he says, *" Following the recruiting sergeant's advice I volunteered for immediate entry only to spend almost a year as a gunner on Ground Defence, a task now undertaken by the RAF Regiment. Still, it was an experience I wouldn't have missed."*

Eventually aircrew training as an Observer commenced with initial training at Scarborough, followed by Bombing & Gunnery School (B&GS), Dumfries, then Air Observer Navigation School (AONS), Bobbington. This took from December 1940 to August 1941 and the final stage was Operational Training Unit (OTU) where crews were formed and finishing touches applied before assessed fit for active squadron service.

It was here, at No. 13. OTU, RAF Bicester, that once again Norman's plans went amiss. Flying Blenheims, he and his crew were on their final assessment flight prior to joining an operational squadron when things went tragically wrong. The aircraft crashed and Norman, the sole survivor, received severe leg injuries which kept him hospitalised for the next eight months, followed by six months recuperating on a ground posting during which he was able to make occasional flights. Finally, passed fully fit for flying, he resumed OTU training on the Blenheim, an aircraft which for him carried unhappy memories.

However it was now 1943 and the Blenheim was ageing as an operational aircraft. More Mosquitoes were coming off the production line and this presented a great opportunity for Norman who found himself switched to complete his training at No.60 OTU, High Ercall, on this extremely versatile aircraft.

A close up view of the Mosquito in flight.

In September 1943 Norman's first squadron posting was to Malta to join No. 23 Squadron at Luqa . The journey involved a two-leg flight leaving from RAF Portreath, a cliff-top field on the North Cornwall coast, to Gibraltar where they had a 24-hour break before continuing to Malta. He describes how on joining the squadron he found he was in for an unsettled time.

"It was the earliest stages of the Italy invasion and we were engaged in ground support of the Army and also carrying out intruder operations over northern Italy. This meant finding strategic targets such as airfields, rail installations and enemy troop movements. Later we found ourselves detached to Sicily to operate from an airstrip on the lower slopes of Mount Etna, perhaps not the most ideal of situations but at least within reach of targets on the mainland . After the Allied landings, and their subsequent advance, it was almost natural we should follow them. We did and found ourselves flying ops from Pomigliano airstrip on the north side of Mount Vesuvious ! Events continued to move swiftly and in December 1943 our detachment from the squadron ended when we returned to join them for their move to Alghero in Sardinia. where we discovered a 1500 feet high mini-mountain rising beside the runway. It was an obstacle we lived with until we left in June 1944 and we never did find out who ordained we should always fly from a mountain side! Our task on Sardinia remained much as before, basically intruder raids on mainland targets but now we also operated occasional sea patrols against German reconnaissance aircraft trailing our convoys. However, there was an extra dimension because from our location we were able to strike at enemy targets in southern France.

Asked about the dangers, Norman tended to brush them aside. *"Nothing can, or should, be said to detract from the seriousness and the sacrifices of those years"*, he said. *"For many, there was a lighter side, fun and games which were a safety valve, a release of tensions, a 'letting off of steam', so necessary to the successful prosecution of the painful duties of war."* As to his own personal experiences he merely added, *"We were lucky. We were often shot at but always avoided being hit. In fact the worst moment was when, due to mechanical troubles, we lost an engine over southern France but fortunately our faithful 'mossie' could fly happily on one!"*

June 1944 saw No. 23 Squadron and Norman recalled to Britain to provide support for the Second Front. Based at Little Snoring, they kept up their assault on the enemy. *"Basically our operations were similar to those we had undertaken in Italy, intruding on enemy airfields and ground attack."* he said. *"We were also much closer geographically to our targets which meant we could spend more time over them, creating havoc where ever we could. During one notable period in August '44, Bomber Command squadrons were 'laid off' for several nights when the whole of Western Europe was cloud free and in brilliant moonlight, greatly favouring the German night fighters, so intruder squadrons of 100 Group were given 'carte blanche' for ground attack operations on railways and road transport systems - great fun!"*

By the time hostilities ended Norman had completed forty ops against enemy targets in Italy and Northern Europe. Post war he remained in the RAF, initially as the Chief Navigation Officer at the Mosquito OTU, RAF Leeming, then in 1949 joining No. 115 Squadron at RAF Mildenhall which operated the Lincoln. However, the following year when the squadron moved, Norman was attached to the USAF at Lakenheath, a role which he describes as 'Maid of All Work', before moving to the Air Ministry in 1951. By now the Cold War was escalating and Norman found himself on a short attachment to the United States to work on contingency planning for pilot training, particularly in view of the introduction of Britain's V-Force. Essential for Britain's defence, it was a task for which he was awarded the OBE.

Following an Air Ministry tour, in 1954 he was given his own squadron, No. 527, based at CSE Watton, Norfolk. This squadron was responsible for calibration of all Early Warning and Fighter Control Radar systems. He operated three Flights, one each of Lincolns, Varsities and Meteors, the latter being replaced later by Canberras.

This was followed by a posting to 83 Group at Wahn in Germany and, later, in 1958, to No. 2 Tactical Operations Centre at Sundern where he was Wing Commander (Planning). Other important appointments during his latter years of service included three years on the staff of the RAF Staff College, Bracknell and three years as Wing Commander (Admin) at Bruggen.

Above: Norman Conquer whilst stationed at RAF Bruggen, Germany,
as Wing Commander (Admin) in 1964.

In February 1968, in his thirtieth year of RAF service, Wing Commander Norman Conquer OBE decided to retire and return to his pre-war profession, becoming a Life Insurance Consultant. A widower, today he lives at Okehampton.

As a footnote, Norman points out the significance of Armistice Day in his flying career. His Blenheim crashed on 11.11.41, his first flight after recovery from injury was 11.11.42 and his first operational sortie was on 11.11.43. All on Armistice Day !

PATH FINDER !

Kenneth H.H. COOK DFC

Ken Cook was born in Gloucestershire in April 1923 and educated locally after which he joined the staff of Sperry Gyroscope Ltd.   However, on reaching the age of eighteen he volunteered for aircrew and was enlisted into the RAF in October 1941.   After preliminary training in the UK and USA he was posted to Canada in July 1942 to commence Air Bomber training at No.31 Bombing & Gunnery School, Picton, Ontario. This was followed by navigator training at No.33 Air Navigation School, Mount Hope, Hamilton, Ontario. On completion of the course in January 1943 he was commissioned as a Pilot Officer and returned to the UK.

After a short period of operational training, in August 1943 Ken and his new crew were posted to No.1661 HCU, Winthorpe, where they initially flew Manchesters before switching to the much superior Lancaster.   On completion of the conversion course they were posted to No.9 Squadron at RAF Bardney, Lincolnshire, at the end of September where he recalls the Squadron motto was "Per Noctum Volamus" which translates as "Flying through the Night". This is what Ken was soon doing as part of Bomber Command's Main Force, with heavily defended Berlin featuring as the target on three of his first ten 'ops'.

However, this early, but successful, baptism had not gone unnoticed and Ken and his crew were 'invited to volunteer' to join the Pathfinder Force (PFF). It was an invitation which they accepted and in December 1943 they were posted to No.8 (PFF) Group via the Navigation Training Unit at Upwood where Ken learned to use the latest navigational and blind bombing radar equipment such as H2S, Loran and Gee. With their training complete the crew joined No. 97 (PFF) Squadron at Bourne on the 19th December 1943 at which time they were regarded as 'beginners'. Ken explains their role both at this stage and later when they became more highly experienced.

"Our tasks were designed to assist the main force squadron aircraft to reach and bomb their targets in a situation where they were still not equipped with the latest radar devices. This entailed us dropping flares to mark the route to the German targets with the object of concentrating the many hundreds of bombers on these raids in space and time.

As we gained experience as a PFF crew we were upgraded to higher grades of competence and responsibility as a target marking crew. When we reached the top grade we carried out the duties of Primary Blind Marker which required us to be one of the first crews over the target and releasing the first group of target indicators precisely on time. After leaving the aircraft these would be exploded in flight on the way to the ground by means of barometric fuses. Seeing these markers would show the main force crews the actual location of the target from up to twenty-five miles away. We also used a variety of coloured flares, green, red or yellow, dependant upon pre-flight briefings and also parachute flares under certain climatic conditions.

On other occasions we would arrive during the attack period when hundreds of the main force aircraft were in the course of bombing the target. Our role then was to re-mark the target when the original markers had burned themselves out. Needless to say this was not particularly popular with us as once the target had been marked we knew German night fighters would be operating in the area."

By April 1944 Ken and his Pathfinder colleagues had been involved in some of the most intensive bomber offensives and against heavily defended enemy targets. These included a further ten raids on Berlin, to add to the three he had earlier undertaken, plus targets at Munich, Essen, Stuttgart, Augsberg and Nuremburg. Ken particularly recalls the latter for this night ninety-three of our bombers were shot down. He was one of those lucky enough to survive ! Once again, his experience was to lead to other things, as he now describes:

" In the April our Squadron, No.97, together with No.83 Squadron from RAF Wyton, were transferred out of No.8 (PFF) Group to a No.5 Group station at RAF Coningsby, Lincolnshire, where they worked on the development of a new marking technique devised by Wing Commander (later Group Captain) Leonard Cheshire VC. Our two heavy bomber squadrons were to 'find' pin-point targets such as German V-weapon storage sites which were frequently located in French railway tunnels."

Ken doesn't say much about his own experiences but the statistics speak for themselves. On June 30th 1944 he was awarded the Distinguished Flying Cross. He was 21 years and 2 months old. A few days later, in early July, Ken and his crew completed a full PFF tour of 45 operations over enemy held territory and were split up to undertake other duties within the RAF. By the time war ended Ken's No.97 Squadron had carried out 381 bombing raids and 49 mine laying raids, a total of 430 raids on enemy targets. This involved their aircraft flying a total of 3398 sorties but the success of their missions did not come cheap. The Squadron lost 124 aircraft but, more tragically, 868 of its airmen failed to return.

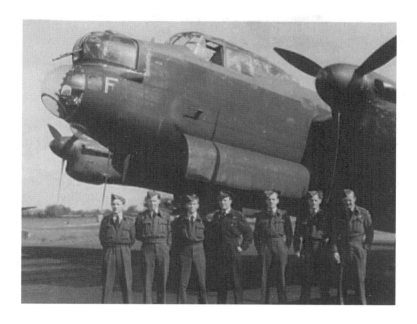

Ken (second left) and the rest of his crew - early 1944

On leaving the Squadron Ken's new role was at RAF Fiskerton where he became the Station Radar Nav Officer which meant he checked the proficiency of all new crews joining the station's squadrons. Then, as war in Europe ended in June 1945 he was posted back to RAF Coningsby in a similar role except this time it was to prepare for 'Tiger Force' - a bomber offensive against Japan. Fortunately war in the Far East ended before it was called into action.

Post war Ken, now a Flt. Lt., remained in the RAF and was granted a permanent commission in 1948. He undertook a number of navigational roles but, always a member of Bomber Command, was surprised when, in January, 1949, his career took an interesting twist. The RAF was re-equipping with their first jet night-fighter aircraft and Ken was posted to No.23 Squadron RAF Coltishall, to fly the Vampire NF10 and later the Venom NF. Promotion to Squadron Leader followed In 1951 and with it a posting to No.228 OCU at Leeming as Chief Ground Instructor to oversee the introduction of the Meteor NF11 and train crews for squadron service in Germany and the Middle East.

In May 1956 he joined No.85 Night Fighter Squadron at RAF West Malling, Kent, as a Flight Commander flying both the Meteor NF11 and 14, later being asked to take command of No.153 NF Squadron which he did with the rank of Wing Commander in September 1957. When West Malling was later closed Ken moved with the Squadron to RAF Waterbeach, Cambs. Here it was re-designated as No.25 Squadron and in early 1959 re-equipped with the Javelin Mk7, a night/all-weather fighter armed with Firestreak air-to-air missiles and 30mm cannon. Later these were replaced by the Mk9 which was fitted with re-heat/after burners.

When Ken's tour with No.25 Squadron ended on the 1st January 1960 he joined a one-year course at the RAF Staff College, Bracknell, which was designed to train senior officers for staff appointments up to Air Rank at the Air Ministry and RAF Command HQ locations at home and overseas. Subsequent appointments saw him serving in Aden and undertaking staff appointments in the UK. However, at the end of 1967, after 26 years service, Ken applied for early retirement to pursue a civilian career as a Director of the National Freight Corporation and later as a Logistics Consultant. Today he enjoys retirement with his wife, Sonia, at Budleigh Salterton.

GLOBETROTTER - from ADDIS ABABA to VANUATU !

Victor R. DABIN

Vic Dabin was born in Bromley, Kent in December 1931, and after leaving Technical College entered the RAF in September 1949, shortly before his eighteenth birthday. Volunteering for aircrew, and after passing the requisite aptitude tests, he was assessed suitable for training as a pilot. Vic undertook initial training at No.1 ITS, RAF Jurby, Isle of Man, before commencing flying at No.7 FTS, RAF Cottesmore. Here he undertook basic flying on the Prentice before progressing to the more advanced Harvard. He was awarded his pilot's wings and granted an 8-year Short Service Commission, on successful completion of the course in September 1951.

Conversion onto jet aircraft followed and for this Vic was posted to No.205 AFS at Middleton St. George, where after dual instruction on the Meteor Mk7 he flew the single-seat Meteor Mk4. Learning the finer arts of aerial warfare followed at No.226 OCU at RAF Stradishall, again flying the Meteor, after which he joined No.245(F) Squadron at RAF Horsham St. Faith, Norfolk. Here he flew the Meteor Mk8, a day fighter version, with the squadron kept on readiness for any hostile intruders from the Eastern Bloc.

The header photograph shows Vic in his Meteor. Note that, whilst the aircraft was fitted with an ejector seat, in the early 1950's pilots still flew in WWII pattern leather helmets. The names painted on the side are those of the ground crew with a responsibility for his aircraft.

Vic left the Squadron in 1954 to join No.121 Wing at Fassberg, and later, Wunstorf in Germany and with it came a change of role. Now, instead of flying Meteors he switched to the Vampire and later the Venom, both fighter-bombers with a ground attack role should Eastern Bloc armour invade Western Europe. However he also had an added responsibility as the Wing Instrument Rating examiner which meant checking all pilots kept current their ability to fly in virtually all weather conditions.

Vic was still in Germany in September 1957 when his Short Service engagement ended and he left the RAF. However, he quickly found a new career with BEA (British European Airways), joining their Viscount 701 fleet as a First Officer. For the next four years he flew their scheduled routes throughout Europe but, whilst accumulating valuable experience of 4-engine aircraft, he was missing the variety and excitement of service flying and in 1961 made the decision to re-enlist in the RAF.

On his return the RAF used Vic's commercial experience to advantage and instead of returning him to the life of a 'fast-jet' pilot posted him to the Far East. Here he joined No.209 Squadron based at Seletar, Singapore, which operated the Twin-Pioneer on short-range transport duties. Whilst only a small number entered RAF service, this versatile aircraft was able to undertake numerous roles, from troop and parachute movements to the carriage of freight. Its particular advantage in being able to take-off and land at the shortest of air-strips made it an ideal transport aircraft in more undeveloped areas. In fact whilst he was at Seletar there was conflict between Malaysia and Indonesia over the former British colony of Borneo. With Britain supporting Malaysia, Vic saw himself detached to support military operations in Borneo on a number of occasions. However, there was also unrest elsewhere in South East Asia and, although Vic does not go into details, it is known he made a number of flights into Laos and Cambodia, all of which entailed a certain element of danger.

With two years operational experience in some of the worst Far East trouble spots, Vic was recalled to the UK where at first he was assigned to instructional duties at No.5 FTS, teaching students on the twin-engine Varsity, before later joining the staff at the Central Flying School. However, in 1968 the Royal Malaysia Air Force was engaged in counter-insurgency operations and sought assistance from the RAF. Once again Vic was heading eastwards, this time 'on loan' to the RMAF. He was given a dual role, flying the familiar Twin-Pioneer also the Herald, and dividing his time between instructing Malaysian students and active operations during which he carried out jungle supply drops and airlifted troops into almost inaccessible landing strips.

Vic returned to the UK in 1970 when, after a short ground tour with the Officer Cadet Training Unit at RAF Henlow, he began a long association with the mainstay of the RAF's Transport Fleet, the Hercules.   This commenced with a posting to No.36 Squadron at RAF Lyneham where he became a Hercules line captain and literally flew around the world. During the next five years operational flying took him to the Far East, Australia and the Americas whilst he also embarked on a number of global 'round the world' training flights. Finally he became a Squadron Commander at the Hercules OCU.

Inevitably a ground tour followed and this was as a Staff Officer at No.38 Group HQ where his knowledge of world-wide operations were put to good use and he became involved in all aspects of air transport policy, from down route handling contracts to aircrew duty limitations and training. However it was not all sitting behind a desk for when pre-independence civil unrest broke out in what later became the Pacific Republic of Vanuatu, then still the jointly Anglo-French ruled condominium of New Hebrides, Vic was detached to the island to arrange the airlift of a stand-by battalion of British troops from the UK in the event of their requirement during the local uprisings.

Returning to operations with the Hercules again in 1980, Vic's first role was as a Hercules Fleet Examiner which not only involved the standardisation and category of Hercules pilots serving with the RAF but those also serving with the Sultan of Oman's Air Force and the Royal Malaysian Air Force which necessitated him visiting both countries.   However, in 1982 the invasion of the Falkland Islands by Argentine forces saw him quickly despatched to Ascension Island as Squadron Leader (Operations).   Here his primary task was the monitoring and supervision of various operational roles in the South Atlantic and included two periods in the Falklands and also one on South Georgia.   Vic describes how he became involved with the latter:

" One of the major problems we faced was the weather which was often extremely unpredictable. The problem arose when, after a 3,500 mile flight from Ascension to the Falklands, we found that we couldn't land because of bad weather and there was no diversionary airfield we could use. Our nearest landfall was Argentina and that was completely out of the question. This meant we had to return to Ascension with our full cargo still on board. In fact I recall that on one such flight I was airborne for   23 hours 45 minutes!   One solution was to see if South Georgia, a mountainous Antarctic island eight hundred miles to the East could provide an alternative. I was despatched there, courtesy of a Royal Navy survey ship, together with a team of geologists and engineers to ascertain whether building an airstrip capable of handling Hercules aircraft was a viable proposition.   My role, as an experienced Hercules pilot, was to give a pilot's opinion.   Our task was relatively easy for there was only one possible site and that was a level area known, ironically,

106

as 'Salisbury Plain'. However this was hemmed in by high mountains and glaciers whilst local gale force winds also added to the problem. My view was that, whilst the actual building of an airstrip was possible, only experienced Hercules pilots should use it and even then with some reservation. For the record - it was never built!"

As operations in the Falklands eased Vic was posted as Squadron Leader Operations at No.1 Group HQ where, once again, he became involved in the world-wide operations of the RAF's Air Transport Force. It was during this tour that he served yet another overseas detachment, this time to Addis Ababa in Ethiopia where he played a significant role in dropping food and supplies as part of the Ethiopian Famine Relief Programme.

With service now drawing to a close, in 1986 Vic became the Technical Editor at the Aircraft Experimental Establishment, Boscombe Down, with responsibility for aircrew publications relating to the Hercules, BA 146, HS 125, Andover and Dominie . With a flying career stretching over thirty-two years, of which twenty-eight were with the Royal Air Force, Vic left the service on retirement in 1987. However, it was not quite the end ! Later that year he took up an appointment in Exeter as the Wing Administration Officer of the Devon Wing of the Air Training Corps, a position he held until finally retiring in 1996.

Today, Vic and his wife, Jill, enjoy retirement beside the Exe at Lympstone.

SOME CONTRASTS of MILITARY FLYING

The Twin Pioneer, illustrated above, was built by Scottish Aviation. Extremely versatile and able to operate from some of the world's roughest and remotest airstrips, it could be used for the carriage of troops, supplies or the deployment of paratroops. Its two 550-hp. Alvis Leonides engines gave official performance figures of a maximum speed of around 165 mph at 2000 feet although normal cruising was around 100 mph.

By contrast you could have crewed the world's first twin-jet aircraft built on a delta platform, the Gloster Javelin pictured above. Designed as an all weather night fighter, it entered squadron service in 1956 and had a maximum speed close to Mach 1 and a service ceiling in excess of 50,000 ft.

ARCHIVE FILM PROTECTOR

Frederick P. J. L. DANCKWARDT

A native Devonian, Fred Danckwardt was born in Devonport in June 1924 and educated at Devonport High School. Hoping to train as a pilot, he volunteered for aircrew and in January, 1943, joined the RAF straight from school. However the recruiting sergeant told him that if he first volunteered as an Air Gunner he would be promised pilot training after completion of his first tour. As Fred says, *" I had no idea what a 'tour' was and on the 16th February I arrived at the Aircrew Reception Centre at St. John's Wood, London, with as lot of other teenage prospective AG's."*

Here things did not go to plan at first and he missed his entry due to extra security checks because of his German surname. He explains, *" My grandfather was interned as an alien in the First World War even though he had two sons fighting for the British, my father in the Royal Artillery and his brother in the Royal Navy. However I joined the next entry which consisted of 'retreads' - serving NCO's and airmen who had volunteered for flying duties. From them I soon learned how to beat the system when necessary!"*

Gunnery training was undertaken at RAF Stormy Down in South Wales where the aircraft used were the Anson and Whitley. The Anson was the first RAF aircraft to be fitted with retractable undercarriage and Fred recalls. *" It took 122 turns on a handle to do this and it always seemed to be my job ! Just to make it more interesting, all the pilots seemed to be Polish who made it quite plain they would rather be on an operational squadron than 'stooging around with sprogs !'*

Next was attendance at No. 16 OTU at Upper Heyford which was equipped with Wellingtons and most of the pilots seemed to be either Australian or ex-Metropolitan

Police Officers.   Fred says he hoped to team up with one of the latter as they seemed 'big and strong' but instead was asked by a short Aussie to join him.   He was Freddie Merrill who'd come to the UK with his brother, an air gunner, but they decided not to fly together to increase the chances that at least one of them would return home.

Completion of OTU led to further training, this time at No. 1661 Heavy Conversion Unit (HCU) at RAF Winthorpe where   initially conversion had been onto the Manchester.   However their engines had proved unreliable and the aircraft had been retired shortly before Fred joined his crew for their conversion onto the Lancaster. Then, on the 1st December 1943, they joined a new squadron being formed at RAF Waddington. Equipped with Lancasters,   this was No. 463 Squadron of the Royal Australian Air Force.

However, there was no rest for Fred as a flu epidemic had hit the station.   Following an urgent call to report to No. 467 Squadron briefing room, he learned he was to fly that night, his first 'op', and he never got to the briefing room in time.   It was an interesting baptism as Fred now describes.

" It was not uneventful as just before we reached our target, Leipzig, the pilot could not contact the Bomb Aimer.   He had disconnected his oxygen, taken off his boots and fallen asleep. Fortunately he recovered in time to drop our bombs but I doubt that he got a good target photo.   It was only afterwards that I learned that this, too, was their first 'op'.   Clearly they improved for after 15 'ops' they went to the Pathfinder Force."

Now flying with his own squadron, there were many more hairy moments to come. Their first 'op' came on the 29th December 1943 when their target was Berlin, the first of four trips they would make to the city.   On their third trip their mid-upper gunner

110

was killed by flak and his subsequent replacement only survived one flight. That was to Leipzig when, once again, they encountered heavy flak and lost all their navigation aids. Despite thick cloud they ultimately landed at Leconfield, albeit with barely enough fuel to turn off the runway. However, over the target their new gunner had completely lost his nerve and on their return was quietly removed from the station.

On 1st March 1944 the target for Fred's eighth op was Stuttgart when his heated suit failed after leaving the target on the homeward leg. A short circuit caused burns to his leg and necessitated his pulling out the heating plug. A Perspex panel had been removed from the turret to improve vision and with an outside temperature around minus-forty he lapsed into unconsciousness with hypothermia and frostbite to the face. He woke up in station sick quarters but passed fit to fly again within two weeks.

The crew's twelfth op was again Berlin when strong winds caused havoc and blew them off course and into the Ruhr's heavy defences on the way home. Freddie, their pilot, had to take drastic defensive measures one of which led to a dive from which they only pulled out through the added strength of both the flight engineer and bomb aimer on the control column. When the aircraft was later examined it was found that the excessive stress had caused the upper wing surface to ripple. It had been a lucky escape.

Some flights were long and one undertaken, to Munich, lasted 9 hours 53 minutes with a route which took them over Lake Como in Italy and across Austria. On the homeward route he and the mid-upper gunner spotted a ME110 about to attack another Lancaster. They both opened fire and saw the enemy go down in flames but as the 'kill' was not independently confirmed it only counted as a 'possible'. By contrast, a short flight followed soon afterwards, only two hours forty minutes, target Lille. Ironically it was to be one of the most dangerous with 20% of the station effort lost.

Of the forty-two aircrew shot down only one survived.

Now highly experienced and battle hardened the crew were selected to fly the RAF Film Production Lancaster. during the latter part of their tour. Fred takes up the story. *"We flew mainly against targets in France and the Low Countries in preparation for the Allied invasion. We carried two cameramen and the aircraft had three cameras, one in a modified front turret, one swung into a window set into the main door and the third swung underneath the aircraft, behind the bomb bay. We also flew with other squadrons, such as No. 617, whenever there was an interesting op. Despite the many hours of combat footage filmed I never saw the results of our work until they were shown in the cinema and of course a lot of use was made of them in later TV programmes."*

Fred completed his first tour with two ops on D-Day, the first in the early hours against the big guns on Utah Beach and again in the evening when the target was the rail network at Argentan when they witnessed a German ammunition train explode. Tour over, there was no respite because his pilot asked the crew to volunteer for another one, flying solely with the Film Production Unit team. It would be a shortened tour filming attacks on interdiction targets in France and Holland.

Finally after forty-four ops Fred was recommended for a commission and on the 21st August 1944 left the base as a Pilot Officer. Ruefully he says, *" Needless to say my promised pilot's course never materialised."* However there was a change of status post war when, after a spell in charge of an Army Review and Interrogation Centre near Hamburg, he applied for an Extended Service Commission. He was subsequently posted as Station Intelligence Officer at RAF Gatow during the Berlin airlift but afterwards was offered re-training as a navigator. This he completed and joined No. 7 Squadron which operated Lincolns.

Other postings followed including a period on Comets at RAF Watton, the role of which was highly classified. Then, in 1967, there was a short ground tour to Aden as the RAF member of the Joint Intelligence Staff prior to British withdrawal at the end of the year. There was also an interesting detachment to Ascension Island to prepare a paper in case the island was ever needed to be used as a staging post. Fred often wonders if anyone ever dusted it off for the Falkland's War .

Sadly Fred's wife died in 1974 and with two young children at school, plus the lack of recent flying posts, he applied for retirement through the RAF redundancy scheme running at that time. Now a Squadron Leader, and aged fifty, he retired after thirty-one years service during which he flew in twenty-two different types of aircraft and visited eighty-two different airfields ! He found a new career with the Department of Health and Social Security and moved to Sidmouth in 1984 on retiring for the second time.

In 1993 Fred was approached by the BBC to participate in a 'Timewatch' programme on Air Intelligence operations which their research indicated he had flown whilst with No's 51 and 192 Squadrons at RAF Watton. On checking with the Ministry Fred found his knowledge still remained 'classified' and he had to decline the invitation.

However if watching TV today, and the programme shows wartime footage of RAF bomber operations, the chances are that Fred was there with his guns protecting the camera !

The Anson, depicted above, was widely used for training navigators, wireless operators and for air gunnery training.

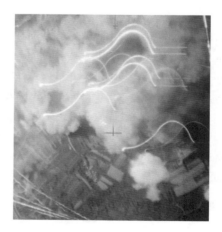

Above: (left) Fred Danckwardt in 1943, aged 19.   Right) An 'aiming point' photograph taken from Fred's aircraft of the airfield and seaplane base at Lanveoc-Poulmic near Brest, France, at 00.01 hours on 9th May 1944.

The white wavy lines indicate tracer fire.

LIFE AS AN AIR ELECTRONICS OFFICER

Ray DODD

Ray Dodd was born in Exmouth in October 1936 but later moved with his family to the outskirts of Chudleigh, close to Teign Valley. As a youngster he experienced seeing a Spitfire chasing an enemy aircraft down the valley and, when war ended, became fascinated by his father's stories. Making model aircraft became a hobby and when, at the age of twelve, his father took him to Exeter Airport for his first flight in a Fairchild Argus he knew there was only one thing he wanted to do when he left school. That was to join the RAF.

As soon as he was old enough he joined the local ATC squadron which opened the door to flying from Exeter in a Tiger Moth and also Anson and Oxford aircraft. At 14 he was gaining experience flying a glider and a year later, too young to enrol as aircrew, decided to enlist as a Boy Apprentice. He arrived at RAF Halton on the 29th April 1952 and after three years training, which he describes as 'second to none', graduated as a qualified airframe fitter. A posting to A&AEE, Boscombe Down, ensued. Here he was introduced to the realities of life after completing a major service on an Anson. He explains.

"The test pilot, who was to fly the aircraft after I'd worked on it, came out of the crew room, looked at me and told me to get a parachute as I was going with him. As the aircraft lifted off the runway I mentally ran through every nut, bolt, cable and rivet that I had put in place and didn't relax until we landed some thirty minutes later."

Ray's stay at Boscombe was, however, cut short when his application for aircrew training was approved although it was with some disappointment that it would not be as a pilot but as a Signaller - the post war term for a Wireless Operator. Training for his new role was undertaken at No.1 Air Signaller School, RAF Swanton Morley and included some 42 hours of practical flying training on Anson and Prentice aircraft. In June 1956 he graduated as a Sergeant Air Signaller and posted to the Maritime Training Unit at RAF St. Mawgan which was equipped with Lancasters, now used for Coastal Command purposes. However moves were already in hand to re-locate the Unit at RAF Kinloss in Scotland, where it would be re-equipped with the Shackleton, so Ray duly travelled North to attend the first course. When this was completed he joined No.42 Squadron which was based at RAF St.Eval and equipped with the Shackleton Mk2. Ray takes up his story:

"My very first flight with 42 Squadron was notable as it ended rather abruptly on the notorious runway 26 with a collapsed tail wheel after a rather spirited flapless landing. We had recently been given a secondary role of Colonial Policing and much training was devoted to this role covering medium level bombing and air-to-ground gunnery. This role took us on several detachments to Southern Arabia, the peak of activity coming in the Summer of 1957. Then we mounted sustained operations in support of the Sultan of Oman's struggle against Saudi backed rebels headed by Talib Bin Ali."

For those who may think flying in peace time lacks those exciting, or perhaps in this case anxious, moments Ray has a tale of a routine flight which will dispel the thought.

"In addition to our normal maritime and search and rescue operations the Shackleton could also be used for the conveyance of troops and with a skeleton crew we could carry thirty-three fully equipped men. It was on such a flight in June 1958 we were tasked with taking a complement of troops from RAF Bovingdon to RAF

116

Nicosia, Cyprus, staging through Malta. With the rest of the crew in their seats I packed the troops in working from the front to the rear and with the last man in the door was closed and I clambered over them back to my wireless operator's position. Just as we were taking off from Bovingdon the rpm on one engine started to fluctuate and the injection boost system had to be cancelled. Suddenly the wooded area at the end of the runway looked huge and there were quite a few white knuckles. Fortunately we didn't realise what a near miss it was until we landed in Malta, Then we found bits of trees in the undercarriage bays."

In October 1958 St.Eval closed and the squadron moved to nearby RAF St.Mawgan where, he says, their highlight was a tour of British Honduras and the West Indies. In the meanwhile Ray had been making applications for re-training as a pilot albeit without success. However, despite his disappointment applications did progress his career in another direction. Airborne technology was advancing rapidly, particularly in relation to the electronic and computer equipment now being installed. In October 1960, after an advanced training course Ray was commissioned as an Air Electronics Officer and posted to No.37 Squadron based at RAF Khormaksar, Aden. Flying the Shackleton Mk2, their role was 'Internal Security'.

When the tour ended in December, 1963, Ray rejoined No.42 Squadron which was still at RAF St. Mawgan and engaged on maritime operations which included keeping a watch on Eastern bloc naval movements. It was also a time when Coastal Command were experimenting with a concept known as 'constituted crews' whereby if one member of the crew was unable to fly the whole crew was stood down. However it was not deemed a success and in June, 1966, Ray left Coastal Command with a move to the Royal Radar Establishment, Malvern. Here he joined the Airborne Radar Group to assist in development of a new maritime radar which culminated in the new Searchwater maritime radar being fitted to the Nimrod Mk1. Another of his projects saw him engaged in high level radar trials on the Vulcan V-bomber based at A&AEE Boscombe Down.

Another twist in Ray's career came in January, 1969, when he was selected to attend the GD Aero systems Course at the College of Air Warfare, Manby, during which he toured both European and North American aviation industries.   On its completion he was retained at the College for the next two years as a lecturer on maritime operations. He then returned to Boscombe, this time as a Trials Project Officer for maritime CA release trials. This was followed by a tour at RAF Lossiemouth with No.8 Squadron on AEW Shackletons   and then a move to HQ No.11 Group at Bently Priory.   Here his remit was to administer to the general requirements of the Airborne Early Warning (AEW) role which included planning for the Nimrod AEW.

Now an acknowledged expert in Airborne Early Warning systems, Ray was seconded to NATO's AEW & Control Programme Management Agency based in the Netherlands as the UK's Nimrod Liaison Officer   This was a joint civil and military procurement agency comprising representatives from thirteen nations subscribing to the AWACS system based on the Boeing E3A, the Nimrod being Britain's contribution.   When in August 1984 the post was disbanded, and the E3A aircraft were being delivered, Ray returned to the UK to continue research at the Royal Aircraft Establishment at Farnborough.

Squadron Leader Ray Dodd left the RAF in May,   1989,   to take up civilian employment as a consultant, later establishing his own computer systems management and support business.

Today Ray lives near Sidmouth with his wife, 'Prim'.

Top: Ray in the back seat of a Prentice whilst undertaking his Signaller training in 1956.

Bottom: Ray, standing on the far right with his 'supercrew' in front of their No.8 Squadron Shackleton whilst based at RAF St. Mawgan in June 1976.

119

LIFE WITH A CHIPMUNK !

John DURRANT M.B.E.

Born in Hertfordshire in January 1925, John Durrant was educated at   Watford
Grammar School and on leaving school volunteered for aircrew at the age of eighteen.
He completed the equivalent of ITW at Durham University Air Squadron in August
1943 and, after grading on Tiger Moths, was selected for further training as a pilot.
However, very soon it became apparent there was a problem with the next phase as he
now explains.

*"In late January 1944 it was off to Scarborough for another refresher or, more
accurately, an advanced winter course in Corporal dodging before a first return to
dreaded Heaton Park at Manchester.   Then it was off to Leuchars in Scotland, not to
fly but to sweep hangars, wash aircraft and be everyone's dogsbody.   Back to
Heaton Park again, only this time to be sent to East Kirby to help No. 617 Squadron
bomb the invasion area.   No, not flying, but pushing their bombs about and more
hangar sweeping.   Once more it was Heaton Park and this time they found a spot for
us at Hornchurch, Essex, to repair V-1 and V-2 damage.   Ironically you could do
nothing about V-2s except to know you'd survived !.   Finally, back to Heaton Park
for the fourth time and, twelve months after passing grading, I found myself down for
a posting to No.5 BFTS at Clewiston in Florida where I would learn more about the
mysteries of Stearmans and Harvards."*

It was now August 1945 and John's was the last course to finish at Clewiston.
Although they now wore pilot's wings they were still far from a squadron posting.
Return to the UK meant an initial posting to Harrogate from where John managed a
move to HQ Flying Training Command where he was given a Harvard and a Corporal

with the role of visiting various units to explain what resettlement facilities were available to those being demobbed.   John succinctly sums up his service by saying, *"I often wonder if any pilot joining in 1943 ever got to squadron service during the war ?"*

John left the RAF in August 1947 and returned to the world of academia. However it was not the end of his flying days. In 1951 he joined the RAFVR at Fairoaks, Surrey, where he completed an Instructor's Course on Chipmunks, then the RAF's basic trainer. Unfortunately in 1954 the Government decided this was an unnecessary expense and the RAFVR flying schools were disbanded. For a while this seemed to herald the end of John's flying but in 1958, quite by chance, he learned of the setting up of the Air Experience Scheme to give flying experience to ATC and other Cadets. He applied and, after a successful interview, became a RAFVR flying instructor and allocated to an Air Experience Flight at Hamble. Little did he realise at the time that this would last until 1990 when he was 'retired' at the age of 65 !

His educational career saw him moving to Devon in 1964 when he was appointed physics lecturer at St. Luke's College, now part of Exeter University, and with it came the opportunity to join No.4 AEF at Exeter Airport.   Many of John's young pupils went on to join the RAF and he recalls how one, after serving as a pilot in a Lightning squadron, came back to join the unit as a part-time volunteer. Many went on to do great things, even attaining Air Rank, whilst others gravitated to become airline captains.

He perhaps sums up his own feelings when he says, *"Thirty-two years flying the same aircraft sounds and is a long time and to have enjoyed every moment is a bonus, as is having both our sons in a Chipmunk. Passing a strict aircrew medical each year was traumatic, especially as one got older, but this was off-set by the opportunity* of attending ATC camps at operational RAF airfields. Held during Easter and Summer school breaks these were the only time we got paid ! My first camp was at Stradishall in 1959 where they flew Hunters and Javelins and my last was in 1990 at the Kinloss Nimrod base. I recall how during the 'Cold War' at least one armed fighter was permanently stationed at the end of the live runway with armed guards never far away to also guard against any IRA threat. None of this affected our Chipmunk flying and 'the old men of 'Dad's Air Force' were unjustifiably looked upon with awe by the jet jockeys. So much so that it was possible to get a ride in almost any type with more than one seat so, through the passage of time, my log book has some unlikely entries"

Surprisingly service with the AEF also provided opportunities for overseas travel and John recalls flights to bases in Germany. "It was a great experience to fly a Chipmunk to Wildenraph and Gutersloh.," he said, "although being refuelled by a cigarette smoking Belgian ground crew at Ostend was a 'stand well back' situation." Of course, things occasionally went wrong and there were unfortunate accidents although John's own record was unblemished. There was the occasional bird strike, or magneto loss but, as he explained, "The Chipmunk is a lovely aeroplane to fly. It rarely bites - but it can do!" But above all he remembers the reactions of the thousands of young men he took through their first flight, from laughter to air sickness - he could write his own book !

By the time John retired records show that he had flown over four thousand cadets, many on their first flight, an enviable record which saw his long period of voluntary service rewarded by the award of the MBE. 1990 also saw his retirement from the education system. Today he lives in retirement with his wife, Lyn, in St. Marychurch, Torquay.

Above: John Durrant (right) with No.4 AEF at Exeter in October 1976.

A De Havilland Chipmunk of the RAF's No.4 AEF based at Exeter.

PRESS ON REGARDLESS.

Ian D. FORBES

Ian Forbes was born in Exeter in March 1921 and educated locally. On leaving school he commenced training as a surveyor before volunteering for aircrew and joining the RAF in March 1942. After initial training in the UK he was despatched to Canada to undertake elementary pilot training on Tiger Moths at No.35 EFTS Neepawa, before progressing to more advanced training on twin-engine Ansons at No.33 SFTS Carberry. Successfully gaining his pilot's wings he returned to the UK and after a year as a Staff Pilot was posted to No.20 OTU Lossiemouth, where he converted onto the Wellington MkX before progressing to No.1663 HCU Rufforth and completing the final stages of training by converting onto the Halifax.

His first operational posting was to an SOE Squadron No.298 at Tarrant Rushton and towards the end of the War in Europe, the whole Squadron was sent to the Far East to take part in a single operation code named 'Zipper'. This operation was abandoned but the Squadron remained in the Far East where it became involved in supply drops in Burma and transport work to Kunming in China, operations which involved long flights over mountainous terrain, very often in monsoon conditions.

How he was selected for this work still remains a mystery to Ian, although his account of an incident whilst at Lossiemouth in December 1944 may give a clue !

Ian was nearing the end of his course and piloting a Wellington Mk.X at the time, having been briefed for a training flight under strict operational conditions. This entailed a flight south to a bombing range near Coventry and returning on an almost reciprocal course to another bombing range near Nairn on the Moray Firth. Also included was air firing out at sea plus other exercises making the flight duration approximately 4 1/2 hours in all. However, the atmosphere before the flight was rather tense and Ian's crew somewhat subdued. Here he explains why.

" A few nights before our sortie a close colleague and his crew were all killed and the following night the other crew in the billet also went down with no survivors. You can imagine the atmosphere in my crew's billet with twelve out of eighteen killed in a couple of nights.

On the day of our sortie we were due for a 1800 hour take-off and during the day I had noticed a build up of cumulous cloud over the Scottish Highlands to the south which formed a solid barrier to our route. The weather forecast was for deteriorating conditions to the South, including rain and snow. Our brief was to fly between 8-12000 feet with six aircraft taking part. My crew were the first to take off and I decided to climb fast before reaching the cloud and I made 17,000 feet hoping to clear the tops. However about ten minutes into the flight my wireless operator reported that other aircraft had been recalled but there had been no signal for us. I told him to check using our call-sign but there was still no response. It was a 'catch twenty-two' situation. Did I turn back because the others had only to find the recall had not applied to me or in best Bomber Command tradition 'carry on regardless'. Having already a thousand flying hours

hours behind me, far more than many of the other pilots, I decided it was meant for me to carry on.   I did but by this time I'd entered cloud and my options had expired. Suddenly the cockpit windscreen turned completely white and the rear gunner called through to say his turret was completely frozen and he was unable to rotate it.   Then the Flight Engineer reported one of the pumps had frozen solid. This only took a few seconds and I also became conscious our airspeed was falling and we were in danger of reaching stalling speed.   By now we were in a steep dive and I was moving the stick backwards and forwards to work the ailerons and rudder to prevent them becoming locked by ice too.   We were quickly approaching 6000 feet when suddenly there was a sound like shrapnel hitting the aircraft.   It was the ice breaking up. Control was regained but although we were now below the cloud we were in inky darkness and in sleet and snow.

We made the first target but decided to avoid the weather front on the return leg, asking the navigator for a course to Aberdeen where, if necessary, I could drop to sea level and into the Moray Firth where the weather would be better.   This we did and happily landed at Lossiemouth about an hour overdue.   Unfortunately our delight was short lived as our aircraft was then invaded by an interrogation team, their first question being why had I ignored the recall signals ?

As a crew we were split up and I was forbidden to have any contact with them. I was paraded before the CO the following morning and on being asked why I had carried on I answered that I understood Bomber Command's unofficial motto was to 'Press on Regardless' and in the absence of any instruction to the contrary this is what I had done.   His reply was to the effect that, whilst that was correct, one should also use their discretion.   Suddenly his demeanour changed and he was once more on Christian name terms.   He told me that our Wireless Operator had been given the previous day's coded call-sign in error and although the tower had received our transmissions they would not answer a wrong call-sign for security reasons. Incidentally, as expected, the recall was due to severe icing conditions,

To this day I do not know whether my actions that day led to my putting up a black in Bomber Command but at the end of out course on the Halifax we were the only crew not to join a Bomber Command Squadron . Instead we were sent to work with the Special Operations Executive . "

Ian was to stay with the same crew for almost two years and when war ended they were engaged on Transport operations. He left the RAF in August 1946 to pursue his chosen career as a Chartered Valuation Surveyor and he later became a Fellow of the Royal Institution of Chartered Surveyors.

However that was not quite the end of the story for in 1949 Ian enlisted in the RAFVR and was able to continue flying with them until the flying element was disbanded in 1954. A further opportunity then presented itself in January 1960 when he became a volunteer instructor with an RAF Air Experience Flight, giving many ATC and other cadets their first experience of flying. It was a role he enjoyed for over twenty six years, until March 1986, when he reached their retirement age. It was a valuable service for which he received the Air Efficiency Award.

Today Ian enjoys retirement with his wife, Joan, close to the banks of the River Teign at Shaldon and continues to enjoy the company of other aviators through his membership of the Torbay branch of The AirCrew Association.

HE GATHERED THE WEATHER.

John Henry GERMAN.

John German was born at Topsham, Devon, in May 1923 and was educated at Exmouth Grammar School. On leaving school in 1939 he joined the former Devon Constabulary as a 'boy clerk' the pre-war equivalent of today's Police Cadet. Whilst serving at Force HQ, then newly built at Middlemoor, he took the opportunity to volunteer for aircrew and was called up in December 1942.

His story is one shared by many who, although commencing training at a time when the losses suffered by RAF aircrews were at their highest, particularly those of Bomber Command, the long avenue of the training process sometimes meant the war in Europe was virtually over before joining their first operational squadron. This was particularly so in the case of trainee aircrew who, because of the over-stretched facilities at home, found themselves sent long distances for flying training in North America or Africa. Nevertheless, their contribution was a vital one.

After initial training in the UK, which included grading on Tiger Moths, John was deemed suitable for further training as a pilot and found himself making the long journey to Southern Rhodesia. The slow route took him on a troopship through the Mediterranean and Suez Canal to eventually reach Durban in South Africa. From there it was a long train ride to EFTS Mount Hampden, near Bulawayo, for elementary training on Tiger Moths before moving on to No.5 FTS at Hean, near Salisbury (now Harare) for more advanced flying on the twin-engine Oxford. With successful completion of training in Southern Rhodesia, John was awarded his pilot's wings and commissioned. However it was not quite the end of his African sojourn for he briefly returned to South Africa for a navigation course before flying to Cairo and from there to Palestine.

The Airspeed Oxford. Used for training pilots on twin engine aircraft.

It was now May 1944 and other vital aspects of training still lay ahead, the next phase being undertaken in Palestine. Here, at No.78 OTU, he began operational training on Wellingtons. However, there was still one last stage and for this John returned to the UK, together with his new crew. Their destination was RAF Aldergrove in Northern Ireland where he attended No.1674 HCU, to convert onto the Halifax four-engine bomber.

In July 1945 John and his crew were given their first squadron posting, to Gibraltar and Coastal Command's No.520 Squadron. Although hostilities in Europe had ceased there was still an important role for their aircraft to play, namely reconnaissance and the gathering of vital meteorological information in an era before the invention of data gathering satellites. For the next eight months, whilst based in Gibraltar, John and this crew were engaged in many such flights which were invariably of long duration and entailed flying vast distances over the Atlantic Ocean. Whilst the dangers of meeting enemy aircraft no longer existed the treacherous Atlantic weather often posed an equally hazardous problem.

129

John German in Palestine - 1944

By early 1946 John's seniority was growing and he was posted back to the UK to undertake a Captain's course. Unfortunately on his return he found no further Captains were required for the time being. The result was he was posted to the cliff-top airfield at RAF St. Eval, Cornwall, to join Coastal Command's No. 179 Squadron.

Here he was to fly a different type of aircraft, the Lancaster, a number of which had been switched from Bomber Command to Coastal Command. However their role was the same as that undertaken by John's last squadron in Gibraltar, namely engaged on vital metrological flights. However, flying from Cornwall meant their area of coverage was much further north where often the weather was even more hostile.

In September 1946 John, who was now a Flt. Lt., left the RAF for civilian street. He briefly returned to the Devon Constabulary but decided a 'policeman's lot' was not for him and opted instead for a career with a large insurance company in the City of London. On retirement in 1984 he returned to his Devonshire roots and now resides with his wife, Eileen, in Exmouth.

PROTECTOR of OUR AIRSPACE

Harold D. 'Griff' GRIFFITH

'Griff', as he likes to be known, was born on the Isle of Man in May, 1929, and after completing education at Douglas High School he opted for a career in the RAF, joining as a Cranwell Apprentice in September 1946. Here his aptitude for learning was recognised when he was sponsored by the Service to read for a degree in Electrical Engineering at Queens University, Belfast. It was here he enjoyed his first real taste of flying for, joining the University Air Squadron, he was soon flying their Tiger Moth and Chipmunk aircraft.

On completion of his degree course his application for pilot training was accepted and, with his primary flying already completed whilst at University, this meant attending No.22 FTS at RAF Syerston to fly Harvards. Advanced training was undertaken at No.207 AFS, RAF Full Sutton, where he flew the Meteor Mks 7 & 4. The final stage came at RAF Stradishall, then No.226 Operational Conversion Unit, where he flew the Meteor Mk8. This was the aircraft he was to fly when he joined his first squadron, No.74, based at Horsham St. Faith and which operated as a day fighter squadron. However this was not their only duty as 'Griff' now explains.

"Basically, being an engineer, it seems whenever the squadron was lumbered with trials I was the one tasked with carrying them out. One of these was testing new airborne VHF homing equipment and entailed trying to find a jamming target. As the endurance of the Meteor was relatively short we had to fly with full wing tanks to extend our flying time to between 1.5 and 2 hours. Eventually the target was found but as we were at 25,000 ft and the jammer, a Lincoln, was at 8,000 feet we were lucky. We had to repeat the exercise three times so the day ended with a sore backside and sore ears through listening to the intense jamming noise all the time.

On another occasion I was tasked with checking the range of the station's 'DME' (Distance Measuring Equipment). I reached the end of its range when I realised I could see the North Frisian Islands off the coast of North West Germany. I then noticed the North Sea was covered with white drifting spray and suddenly became aware of how lonely it was and how important the noise of the engine had suddenly become. We normally flew in pairs over the sea but on this occasion I was alone."

For those who wonder whether service aircraft are subject to HM Customs clearance when returning from overseas, 'Griff' provides this anecdote.

"We'd just completed a two week detachment in Holland and were preparing to leave when the weather closed in. As it was the Thursday before the Easter weekend all the ground crew had been flown out in the morning and I was responsible for re-crystallising the Squadron's twelve aircraft. I led the last section home, flying below cloud at 500 feet and when we landed the ground crews were rushing to put the aircraft away and disappear for their weekend break. It was then that a young Customs 'junior' espied a hatch under the fuselage and demanded to inspect the space behind it. The ground crew opened it and he climbed inside. Then a different flight crew, seeing the open hatch and wishing to help their colleagues, promptly

132

closed and fastened it and then wheeled the aircraft into the hanger. Over an hour passed and the senior customs officer realised his junior was missing. A search was instigated and, opening the already closed hanger doors, we could hear the frantic knocking. Junior was released. He was lucky, he could have been there all Easter!"

When he finished his tour with No.74 Squadron, the RAF decided that Griff's engineering experience was more useful to them in other ways . Considerable advances were being made in the fields of aviation electronics and radar and he was posted to the Royal Radar Flying Unit to undertake various trials at Defford and Pershore. Whilst here he extended the types flown to include the Devon, Canberra and Hastings. Being so involved with the technical aspects of aircraft equipment, which he says can be quite boring for most, Griff tends to concentrate on the more humorous incidents like the couple he now relates.

"The Canberra is inherently cold to fly in, particularly at high level. In fact it has been described as English Electric's flying 'fridge. You can imagine the amusement when one day a 'boffin' turned up for a high level sortie fully dressed in sweaters, flying overalls and heavy gloves. The problem? He was also wearing open toed sandals with no socks ! On another occasion I was flying as co-pilot on a Hastings . When the 'boffins' arrived they were carrying large thermos flasks and we immediately thought we'd have lots of hot tea or coffee during the flight. How wrong we were, the sorties was for trials of intra-red detectors and the flasks were full of liquid nitrogen !"

Gradually the flying experiments became fewer as 'Griff' became ever more involved with the development of radar systems, beginning with a posting in 1960 to HQ Electronic Systems Command. His experience in this aspect of the Nation's defence was further enhanced when he was posted to the United States as the UK Liaison

Officer for the USAF Ballistic Missile Early Warning System (BMEWS) Programme Office. Its sole aim was to provide an early warning system based on the expected path of inter-continental ballistic missiles coming from Europe over the Arctic before impact in the US. This led to warning radars being installed in Alaska, Greenland and the UK, the latter becoming the well known site at Fylingdales on the North Yorks Moor. *"We knew it was for providing us with a four minute warning against nuclear attack but for the Americans it was ten minutes"*, he said.

In fact 'Griff' was in the US when the war threatening 'Cuban Missile Crisis' escalated and presented the US with a new problem. This was how to provide an effective warning for a missile launched from much nearer home, in this case from Cuba. Much brainstorming took place and 'Griff' was co-opted as a full member of the team. As expected, the USAF went onto a high state of alert. Fortunately the crisis was defused by diplomacy but this did not stop work continuing behind the scene.

Between 1970-73 he served at RAF Gibraltar as OC Engineering but most of his later work has remained 'classified'. All we can say is that his involvement with early warning systems made western skies much less vulnerable to airborne attack throughout the Cold War. After almost 38 years RAF service, and now a Squadron Leader, he retired in May 1984. He was subsequently employed by the UK Division of Rockwell-Collins as a Programme Manager responsible for systems programmes concerning the Company's air defence speciality of Tactical Data Links. In the US, its parent company was responsible for various projects including NASA's Space Shuttle and the GPS Satellite system.

Now fully retired he lives in Budleigh Salterton with Valerie, his wife.

AIRCREW LIVES SAVED BY NAVAL HEROES.

Deryck W. GROOCOCK AFC

Deryck was born in Leeds in June 1922 and educated locally. Leaving school he entered the family business of Provision Merchants but couldn't wait until he was eighteen and able to enlist in the RAF. In the meanwhile he served for two years, between August 1938 and September 1940 in the Air Defence Cadet Corps.   With maths and physics amongst his matriculation subjects, he was selected for training as a pilot and on the 2nd January 1941 arrived at an Aircrew Reception Centre in Babbacombe. ITW was undertaken at Newquay and then it was a long journey across the Atlantic for flying training.

Once in the US Deryck joined Class 42A at the US Army Air Corps Flying School at Lakeland in Florida. It was incidentally the first course in the US under the 'Arnold Scheme' which was named after the US General who conceived it.   Training in the US was on the PT17 Stearman, the   BT13 Vultee and, finally the AT-6 Harvard. Uniforms were not worn by RAF personnel as the US was not, at that time, at war although it was later, having been attacked by the Japanese at Pearl Harbour a few weeks before Deryck sailed home.

The PT-17 Stearman,
widely used in the US
as a primary trainer

The voyage home has, however, remained etched in his memory as he now relates:

"We were sailing home in a fast convoy of two merchant ships with an escort of four Royal Navy destroyers. We were constantly under attack by packs of German submarines whilst off the eastern coast of the United States and on the third night one launched a torpedo straight towards our ship. One of the escort destroyers, seeing the danger, darted between us and took the torpedo itself in order to save the hundreds of trained aircrew aboard. There were no survivors from the destroyer; the Navy have been heroes to me ever since."

Arriving safely home, Deryck was destined to join Bomber Command and after OTU at Harwell, where he flew Wellingtons, he was posted to operations in the Middle East. However the flight to Cairo was far from routine. Many aircraft had been lost to enemy air attacks whilst making transit stops in Malta so the new route was via Gibraltar, Bathhurst, Lagos and then across Africa before flying up the Nile towards Egypt. Deryck reckons there wasn't much of a saving as many of the crews got lost in the desert ! Finally, on arriving in Cairo he learned there would be a long wait before a squadron posting came through so, on hearing volunteers were needed to fly an aircraft to India, he persuaded his crew to join him having been assured they would come straight back.　Deryck takes up the story.

" We duly arrived at Digri, in Assam, which was the home of No.99 Squadron, and asked how we would get back to Cairo. We were told that a tour in India for a single man was four years. It was a shock but they were right and we stayed with No.99 Squadron.　Flying Wellingtons, we attacked Japanese held airfields, marshalling yards and troop concentrations in Southern Burma and also shipping along the coast."

Many aircrew will say that survival was a matter of luck and many lost friends. Here Deryck looks at the odds.　*"I flew as 2nd pilot for these ops, a newly promoted 2nd pilot being added to the crew as Captain and my old 2nd pilot was put with another crew.　For some reason I was sent to Bombay for a shipping recognition course and on my return I was saddened to learn my crew had been posted as 'missing'. A few nights later I heard a terrific explosion on the runway. A returning Wellington had landed but, unknown to its crew, its primed bomb load had failed to release and was hanging below the closed bomb doors.　My old 2nd pilot was with the crew so now I was the only one of the six who had left the UK together to be still alive."*

Today Deryck would be the first to admit that he didn't like flying the Wellington for, being a single-engine pilot at heart, he found the aircraft under-powered, heavy and lumbering. It was not surprising, therefore, that when volunteers were sought to fly the Blenheim he immediately applied. This meant attending an OTU on the North West Frontier before being posted to join No.60 Squadron which moved to Madras shortly after his arrival. From there he carried out a few more anti-shipping patrols before moving again, this time to Bangalore. Here he learned that pilots were to be converted by No.135 Squadron to fly the Hurricane Mk IIc. At last Deryck's dream was coming true and he had about ten hours flying time on the famous fighter when he succumbed to a bad case of hepatitis and was hospitalised. By the time he recovered the squadron had fully converted and moved on to fly operationally. He was left in limbo.

Eventually he was posted to No.194 Squadron which operated Dakotas. Initially based near the North West Frontier, it moved to Assam soon after he joined them. Describing his new squadron as a 'happy one', Deryck was also full of praise for the Dakota which, he said, unlike the Wellington, was light to fly and could be thrown around almost like a fighter!

The DC -3 Dakota which was widely used for troop and supply drops.

Spending the next eight months flying over inhospitable and often mountainous country, he was recently asked about the type of operations they flew and whether there were any anxious moments to which he replied:

"We flew three or four sorties a day, dropping supplies to the 14th Army on several fronts including the Box at Arakan and the Battle of Imphal. At the same time we were supporting Wingate's Chindits, flying them in and out of small airstrips behind the Japanese lines. We also kept them supplied and amongst more unusual cargoes I carried were mules and oxen, the latter being killed for food. On return flights we would repatriate any wounded. I suppose we had many close shaves

but one was particularly close.   We were flying at 8,500 feet but as the range of hills below were at 7000 feet our actual clearance was only 1500 feet. and to make matters worse there was a solid layer of stratus cloud between us.   We were nearing our drop zone and I was looking for a gap through which we could descend, find the DZ and make our drop. I told the crew to go back and prepare for dropping but as they did so the air speed started to fall for no apparent reason.   I increased power but it continued to fall at an even faster rate.   Suddenly the aircraft reared up and went into a left-hand spin and I knew I only had 1500 feet to effect a recovery before we crashed into a mountain top.   I tried to correct the spin and watched the altimeter quickly winding down , passing the 7000 feet mark and expecting us to crash at any moment.   Then at 4,600 feet I regained control as we burst through the cloud layer.   There, towering above us on either side , were the mountain peaks. We were in a valley.   Furthermore, ahead of us we saw the smoke marking the drop zone.

It later transpired that of the twelve aircraft which set out for the drop we were the only one which actually found the mark, a feat which earned the praise of the army commander. Little did he know what a close thing it was. As for the problem with the aircraft, it was almost certainly due to the load being placed too far back near the door and affecting the centre of gravity. It was a mistake we didn't make again. "

Following completion of his operational tour, Deryck spent the next fifteen months as a VIP pilot with the Communications Squadron based at Delhi.   Here his many VIP passengers included Lord Mountbatten, General Auchinleck and General 'Boy' Browning before he became the personal pilot to Air Chief Marshal Sir Leslie Hollinghurst, the Base Air Forces S.E. Asia Commander.   It was during this period he was awarded the Air Force Cross for, he says, *"never being turned back by monsoon weather even though it was rather scary at times !"*

Deryck left the RAF in January 1947 but remained in the RAF Reserve of Air Force Officers whilst trying civil flying. He rejoined again in May 1949. Qualifying as a Flying Instructor his post war career saw him instructing in Southern Rhodesia and, entering the 'jet age', flying Meteors at the Central Fighter Establishment where he was training Instrument Rating Examiners. A Staff posting in Germany followed where he flew both the Meteor and the Vampire on his staff visits. Later he attended a course at the RAF Staff College. Another two year spell of flying followed, this time with his appointment as OC Beverley Squadron at No.242 OCU, Dishforth.

In a career which was to last some thirty four years, Deryck had many more important appointments during his latter years, including Deputy Station Commander at RAF Brize Norton, the RAF's largest air base and where, incidentally, he learned to fly the VC-10. His last appointment of all was as the Station Commander at RAF Swinderby.

The VC-10 flown by Deryck whilst deputy Station Commander at RAF Brize Norton 1972-1973

However ask him what was his most enjoyable posting and he will reply without hesitation, *"my two and a half years in Ottawa as the Air Advisor to the British High Commissioner and senior Royal Air Force Officer in Canada."*.

Having reached the rank of Group Captain, Deryck retired from the RAF in 1974 and today enjoys a peaceful life in Sidmouth with his wife, Elizabeth.

SCARIEST MOMENTS WERE DROPPING FOOD !

Adrian HEAL

Adrian Heal is a Cornishman, born at St. Blazey in April 1925, and after being educated in Camborne commenced work as a wages clerk with the Cornwall Electric Power Company.   Aged just eighteen, in July 1943 he joined the RAF and volunteered for aircrew.   He was then selected for training as a Wireless Operator and posted to No.2 Radio School at RAF Yatebury before continuing the training process at an Advanced Flying Unit at RAF Wigtown in Scotland.   Finally, now proficient as a Wireless Operator, came the stage of joining a crew prior to a squadron posting. This was at the Operational Training Unit, RAF Chipping Warden, on the twin-engine Wellington bomber. From there we went to the Heavy Conversion Unit (HCU) at Woolfox Lodge, Rutland, flying the larger four-engine Lancaster.

It was 1944 when Adrian and his new colleagues joined their first squadron which was No.195 and operated Lancasters from RAF Wratting Common.   Reminiscing about those far off days, Adrian's main thoughts are of the tremendous camaraderie which existed between the close-knit crew.

"I was just twenty and the youngest of our crew when we flew our first op," he says. *"In fact I used to think of them as the brothers I never had although we were quite a mixed bunch from all over England and Wales.   We lived together, flew together and always went out together - just like a big happy family !"*

Later when Adrian was asked about his operational flying he replied,   *"Well I think the fact that we were such a close crew helped, together with a lot of luck.   We flew a number of missions including six of the major bombing raids on the German*

141

heartland itself but always came through unscathed. In fact our most nervous moments came whilst not on a raid at all.

The war was in its final throes and the civilian population of Holland and Belgium were in desperate need of food and other vital supplies. Somehow a special arrangement was made with the Germans for us to fly over territory still occupied by them to make relief drops. In our case we were to carry these out over Belgium. The frightening moments came when, flying low and slow over their territory, we wondered if they would keep their word. To their credit, they did. Nevertheless, we were glad to get out of there."

An Avro Lancaster in the act of taking-off.

Adrian participated in a number of these 'Manna' drops and three days after his last one the war officially ended. However, there were still a number of tasks which the bombers could undertake and for a while Adrian was engaged in flying home our liberated POW's from France and Italy.

Although the war in Europe was now over the threat in the Far East still remained and after eighteen months together Adrian's close-knit crew from No.195 Squadron was posted to another Lancaster squadron, No.9 Squadron based at RAF Waddington. This was part of the RAF's newly conceived 'Tiger Force' whose role it would be to

142

undertake the bombing of mainland Japan.   Fortunately we know that hostilities in the Far East came to a swift end with the dropping of A-bombs on Hiroshima and Nagasaki and 'Tiger Force' was never called into action.   Despite the sudden ending of the war against Japan, Adrian still found himself heading eastwards with his crew to RAF Salbani, near Calcutta.   He admits there was little to do there and within three months he was heading homewards again.

Adrian standing second from right with the rest of his Lancaster crew.

Adrian was demobilised in February 1947 and joined the former Plymouth City Police Force, retiring after twenty-five years service to start a new career with the Foreign Office.   Engaged in Embassy security, he spent the next ten years serving at the British High Commission at Kampala in Uganda and Embassies in Sofia, Helsinki, Geneva and Bonn.   Today, their travelling over, Adrian and his wife, Pauline, live quietly in Plymouth where he is a member of the local branch of the AirCrew Association.

143

'HE WEIGHED ONLY SIX & A HALF STONE!'

Stanley HURRELL

Stan Hurrell was born in Paignton in November 1920 and educated at Totnes Grammar School from where he joined the Post Office as a junior clerk. Aged nineteen, he joined the RAFVR in early 1940 and was initially trained at RAF Yatesbury as a wireless operator (ground) after which he was posted to their SHQ Signals unit.

He applied to re-muster as aircrew at the end of 1941 and the above photograph was taken at that time. He progressed via No.4 ITW at Scarborough to No. 6 ETFS, Sywell. Here he was reclassified for training as a Bomb Aimer which saw him undertaking bombing training at Wigtown before joining a new crew at No. 10 OTU Abingdon in September, 1942. Here they flew Whitleys and Stan recalls a flight they made alone on the 12th January 1943.

" *Our job was to drop leaflets on Paris but we also carried boxes containing strips of tinfoil which were shoved down the flare chute all the time we were over enemy territory. We didn't treat it very seriously but nevertheless were thankful to have been totally unmolested by enemy throughout the flight. On our return we found the whole of S.E. England blanketed in fog but luckily spotted flares and landed safely in Wiltshire almost out of fuel,* "

After OTU Stan and his crew were posted to No. 1658 CU at Ricall to convert onto the four-engine Halifax Mk 11b before joining No. 78 Squadron at Linton on Ouse on 28th March 1943. Four days later they were to fly their first 'op', a raid on St. Nazaire of which he proudly says they were the only one out of twenty three aircraft from their station to bring back a photograph spot on the target. Their second operation came on the night of 10th April 1943 when the target was Frankfurt am Main and things went horribly wrong as he explains:

The Handley Page Halifax Mk2, series 1.

"We were intercepted by a Messerschmitt 110 near Metz and attacked from below. We only spotted him an instant before he opened fire and were hit on the underside of the starboard mainplane. Both starboard engines were knocked out and the wing set on fire. The fire extinguishers were not effective in putting out the blaze which grew very fast. We tried to jettison the bombs but the skipper had to countermand the order and tell us to get out fast, which we did. I believe the enemy fighter came in again and we learned later that Jethro, one of our gunners, had been killed. The aircraft crashed near the village of Anoux, north west of Metz. The rest of us survived but I only managed to evade capture until late afternoon on Sunday, the 12th. Eventually we were all taken prisoner and with the exception of our navigator,

145

who was sent to Sagan, we all ended up in a POW camp at Barth and were to spend the next two years in German hands"

A Me 110 similar to the one which shot down Stan's Halifax near Metz on the 10th April 1943.

Many accounts have been written of POW experiences and tell stories of comradeship but also despair and deprivation.   Here Stan tells his:

"Our interrogation at Dulag Luft, Frankfurt, was stressful, as was the civilian reaction to us outside Frankfurt railway station. However, we found Barth better than we expected, with plenty of activity and enough to eat thanks to the wonderful Red Cross. From Barth we travelled east to Heydekrug on the border between East Prussia and Lithuania.   It was a sad comedown for us.   It was horrible and by the time we left in July 1944 we were sick and very hungry.   Of the 7000 POWs in the camp half went by sea from Memel to another camp at Gross Tychau in Poland but I was with the others who went by cattle truck to Thorn (Torun), also in Poland. We were only there four weeks during which time most of us contracted dysentery because of the awful water supply.   Then we were moved again, this time by rail to

Fallingbostel in NW Germany, next door to Bergen-Belsen, although thankfully we knew nothing of the concentration camp at the time. The winter of 1944-45 was dreadful. I was not very big - at Totnes Grammar School I was called 'Tacker' - but by liberation I weighed no more than six and a half stones. However it was the bigger lads who suffered most and, sadly, not all of them made it back home.

The Allied armies were close at hand by 5th April 1945 when the Germans tried to move us eastwards towards Lubeck where a large accumulation of Red Cross food was being held, but we never reached them. Monty's Eleventh Armoured Brigade released us in the village of Wendischevern, near Luneberg at 4.25 pm on Wednesday, 18th April `1945. Next day another large collection of struggling POWs stopped for some food in the village of Gresse, a few miles away, and were strafed by seven Typhoons. Over thirty died there. There were other incidents in the area but perhaps inevitable that such things happened. Everything was in chaos."

Stan arrived back in England on the 24th April and two days later met up with his sweetheart, Christine, at Birmingham New Street Station. They were married at Totnes less than two months later, on the 16th June 1945. In the August Stan left the RAF and returned to his job with the Post Office rising to become PO Controller in London.

Retiring in 1979 he wasted little time in returning to his Devonshire roots and today lives in Ivybridge. This year, 2005, he and Christine will have been married for sixty years, a fact summed up by Stan who says, *"What a fortunate lad I was"*.

In April 1996, on the 53rd anniversary of being shot down over Anoux, Stan returned to the scene thanks to the initiative of a retired French Air Force colonel, meeting villagers and visiting the grave of their gunner, Jethro.

ADVISOR to the MOVIE MAKERS !

Michael JENKINS

Born in Birmingham in 1931, Mike was educated at Sebright School, Wolverley, Worcestershire. It was whilst still at school that he decided upon a career in the RAF and initially joined as an apprentice engineer from school in 1947 . However later he was given the opportunity of training as a pilot and granted an 8-year Short Service Commission. His aircrew training began at No.1 ITS, RAF Jurby, Isle of Man, following which Mike was posted to Southern Rhodesia, now Zimbabwe. Stationed at No.5 FTS, Thornhill, his basic flying was carried out on Tiger Moths before progressing to the much more advanced Harvard. Awarded his pilot's wings, on return to the UK he converted onto jet aircraft at No. 205 AFS, RAF MIddleton St. George, where he flew Meteors, before   undertaking operational training at No.226 OCU, RAF Leeming, where he teamed up with his navigator to fly Meteor NF11 night-fighters,

In 1953, after successful completion of his course at OCU, Mike joined No. 96 Squadron which was then based at RAF Ahlhorn, Germany, as part of No. 2 Allied Tactical Air Force (ATAF). Although it was the time of the 'Cold War' Mike says, *"there was a bit of a lull whilst I was there although it heated up after I returned to the UK"* In 1959 he was posted to No. 64 Squadron based at RAF Duxford, an airfield known to many as it is now part of the Imperial War Museum. Here he continued flying the Meteor NF11 and its later variant the NF14. Then, after the squadron re-equipped, he flew the delta wing Gloster Javelin which was the RAF's first aircraft designed specifically to undertake both all-weather and night-fighter roles.

Leaving No.64 Squadron at the end of his tour it was almost inevitable that a ground tour would follow and for Mike this meant a posting to HQ Fighter Command as Personnel Officer. However, in 1961 it was overseas once more, this time to join No.48 Squadron based in Singapore at RAF Changi. This also heralded a role change for, following a conversion course, Mike was now switched from fighters to Transport Command and his new squadron was equipped with the Hastings, a four-engine long-range transport aircraft.

Above: The Handley Page Hastings.

Remaining with the Squadron until 1964, during which time he became a Flight Commander and was promoted to Squadron Leader, Mike outlines some of the roles they undertook at that time.

"Changi was a hub on the RAF's transport route between the UK and Japan so we would fly part of that route. However we also became involved in the confrontation between Malaysia and Indonesia in Borneo. The UK sided with Malaysia, mproviding manpower and logistical support. which meant supplying troops in Borneo by a variety of means, including air drops. On a personal note, whilst at Changi I also had the role of Squadron Training Instructor on the Hastings."

Although the Hastings was to remain in service until late 1967, its long-range role ceased when the new Bristol Britannia arrived at RAF Lyneham in 1957. The Britannia was to play a major role in RAF Transport Command for almost twenty years, being finally withdrawn from service in 1976. However it was a role shared with a new arrival to the UK in December 1966 when the first of the US-built Lockheed Hercules aircraft arrived to be based also at Lyneham.

After a tour at MoD and another overseas tour running the Joint Operations Centre in Bahrain, and promoted to Wing Commander, Mike first undertook a conversion course on the new Hercules at RAF Thorney Island before being posted to Lyneham as the OC Ops Wing.

Modified and with derivations, the Hercules still remains the linchpin of RAF transport operations almost forty years after its first arrival. For a period Mike instructed crews on the Hercules and now describes some of the tasks he undertook with the aircraft.

"One of the main advantages of the Hercules was its ability to carry a large number of troops and facilitate the dropping of parachutists. Of course this required extensive co-operation between the RAF and the Army and also intensive training on both sides. You could almost say it was a specialist role but it was also one with which I became very much involved. In 1971 I became parachute trained

and subsequently spent 2 1/2 years with No.16 Parachute Brigade. At least when they jumped from my aircraft they couldn't say I didn't know what they were doing !"

Above: A Lockheed C-130 Hercules silhouetted against an evening sky
as it comes in to land at RAF Lyneham, Wiltshire.

Interestingly Mike's parachuting came to good use a couple of years later, in 1976 when the epic motion picture 'A Bridge Too Far', the story of the ill-fated 'Operation Market Garden' at Arnhem, was being filmed.   To re-create the scenes not only did they need scores of parachutists but also the Dakota aircraft which were used in the original campaign.   Whilst the British Army's Parachute Brigades could provide the former, the aircraft initially provided a problem.   Fortunately the Finnish and Danish Air Forces still operated a number of Dakotas and were prepared to provide them. However, now another problem arose because at that time, the Ministry of Defence would not allow our troops to fly in foreign aircraft unless all operational and safety aspects were checked by British aircrew .   So, whilst the film was in the making Mike found himself in the role as 'Service Advisor' to Sir Richard Attenborough (as he was then).

Between 1976 and 1981 Mike sums up his career as being *'a number of staff appointments'* and as a Wing Commander with thirty-fours years RAF service, the prospects of another flying tour were diminishing so he decided to retire and pursue his flying elsewhere. He flew the C130 Hercules with the Sultan of Oman's Air Force on a four-year contract.

As one door closed another opened and when Mike's contract in the Oman ended he remained in the Middle East for a further four years, switching to the commercial environment when he joined Saudi Arabian Airlines as a Chief Instructor Flight Safety Training. In 1989 he left Saudi to return to the UK for further appointments in the field of aviation.

A qualified Flying Instructor and examiner, both for private and commercial pilots, he undertook a number of assignments over the next fourteen years, one of which reminded him of his days with the Parachute Brigade in the 1970's. In 1996 he became a QFI for Army Air Corps pilots at Middle Wallop!

Today Mike is officially retired and lives on the Devonshire border at Uplyme with his wife Pat. However it cannot be said he has given up flying for he owns his own aircraft which he keeps at Dunkeswell, So, if you see a Piper Arrow overhead it could well be Mike !

HE DITCHED IN ICELANDIC WATERS

Samuel B.V. JOHNSON

Born near Crewe, Cheshire, in February 1919, Sam Johnson won a scholarship to Nantwich Grammar School after which his love of rural life saw him engaged in farm work.   However, when war came he was willing to leave the land and enlist in the RAF, volunteering for aircrew. Now aged twenty-one, he was subsequently selected for the combined role of Wireless Operator and Air Gunner (W/Op.AG) and after basic training attended the Wireless Operators' Course at the RAF Signal School, Yatesbury. In March 1941 he continued with further training at No.7 Bombing & Gunnery School, Stormy Down, which incorporated flying on the Fairey Battle and Whitley.   Advance stages followed during the late Spring of 1941 with further training at Prestwich and attendance at No.3 COTU at Silloth.

The Whitley.

His first operational posting came soon afterwards when he joined No.612 Squadron on the 13th August 1941. Part of Coastal Command, it was then operating Whitleys from Wick although in January 1942 they relocated to Reykjavik in Iceland to continue their primary role of anti-submarine patrol and convoy escort.   However the North

153

Atlantic was not a friendly place, particularly in winter, as Sam was to discover on the 17th March 1942 when, operating from their Icelandic base, their aircraft was forced to ditch in the ocean, an incident he now recalls:

"We were some 400 miles out from Iceland and engaged on a routine anti-submarine patrol and convoy escort. We were flying over the ocean at about 2000 feet but still had some way to go before reaching the convoy and I was in my normal rear turret position at the time. It was then I saw a peculiar cloud appearing over the wing. I called the skipper on the intercom and our navigator took a closer look from the astrodome to discover a glycol leak from the starboard engine . Mind you our aircraft was a 'chuck-out' from Bomber Command and though it had been reconditioned it was still really a 'heap of crap'.

The leak appeared serious and the skipper decided to return to Iceland. We managed to make some height before the engine packed up and then we started to lighten the aircraft by jettisoning heavy items such as our depth charges. The skipper spent the next four hours nursing our crippled aircraft homewards. We almost made it when, only twelve miles from the Icelandic coast, the other engine stopped. We had no option but to go down. Our distress calls had been picked up by a patrolling Hudson and they watched as our skipper make a great job of ditching, albeit with a big splash !

We managed to get into our dinghy which was half full of water. It was very cold, only 4 or 5 degrees. We watched our aircraft sink, its port wing rising in the air as it submerged beneath the waves. It was a sad sight but we were fortunate not only to survive but to be picked up within a couple of hours by an Icelandic trawler which took us back to land."

154

It was whilst based in Iceland that Sam volunteered for 'TRANSAT', an operation designed for ferrying USAAF B-17F Flying Fortresses across the Atlantic for use in European operations. Flying via Newfoundland they would pick up a RAF wireless operator in Iceland for the final stage of the journey and Sam made three such flights before another posting came through. This involved a short stay at RAF Chivenor where No.172 Squadron were operating the Leigh-light Wellington which used airborne searchlights to hunt U-boats at night. After familiarisation with their operation Sam moved on to join No.179 Squadron based in Gibraltar which operated the same modified Wellingtons. Arriving on 'The Rock' in February 1943 he completed his tour with them six months later by which time his log book showed over five hundred flying hours - he doesn't mention his Icelandic trawler time ! Their maritime patrol duties had encompassed a large area of the Mediterranean and the Bay of Biscay.

After completion of his operational tour Sam was initially posted as a radar instructor at RAF Hooton Park where he was also commissioned. Further instructional duties followed at RAF St. Athan before a final posting to the Empire Radio School at Debden. Here he became both Signals and Radar Leader and later was to be in charge of the Air Operating Section.

Now a Flt. Lt., in March 1952 Sam was seconded from the RAF to the fledgling British European Airways for a six month period as a Wireless Officer. On completion of the secondment he returned to the RAF and was demobilised in the September. He subsequently undertook a variety of civilian occupations which included becoming a Publican and Hotelier and skilled work as an Instrument Engineer.

Sam finally retired in 1983 since when he has lived with his wife, Joan, in the Dartmoor fringe village of Sparkwell, near Plymouth.

A member of the elite 'Goldfish Club' whose membership is restricted to those who have *' escaped death by the use of his Emergency Dinghy'* Sam also has a couple of photographs to remind him his 'lucky day'.

Top: A dramatic photograph taken by the Hudson crew as it circled overhead following their 'May Day' call. The crew's dinghy can just be seen to centre right of the picture. Bottom: Sam, (far right) pictured with his crew shortly after their rescue.

FROM TIGER MOTH TO V-BOMBER

Trevor W. OAKEY AFC

Trevor Oakey was born in Birmingham in October 1924 and after a grammar school education started a career in the Inland Revenue Department of the Civil Service. However at the age of eighteen, and with the war at its height, he volunteered for aircrew and was called to RAF service in April 1943. Assessed suitable for pilot training he undertook his initial induction course in the UK before undertaking the long journey to Canada where he was posted to No.33 EFTS at Caron in Saskatchewan. Here flying was undertaken on the Fairchild Cornell, a low wing monoplane which was built in the USA as a primary trainer and had two cockpits set in tandem. Advanced flying followed at No.34 SFTS located at Medicine Hat, Alberta, where Trevor flew Harvards.

During his flying training in Canada Trevor showed exceptional skill as a pilot which was to have a significant effect on his future career for, instead of returning to the UK, he was retained in Canada where he qualified as a Flying Instructor . He remained there until 1945, instructing pupils on Harvards at No.6 SFTS, Dunville and No.16 SFTS at Haggersville, Ontario. Even then his days as a Qualified Flying Instructor (QFI) were far from over. On return to the UK he continued this role at two home based Flying Training Schools.

He was demobilised in 1947 and attended University at Durham where he obtained a B.Sc in Geology. However his graduation in 1950 coincided with an escalation of international tension with both the 'Cold War' and the North Korean invasion of South Korea which triggered the Korean War. It was a period when the RAF were short of aircrew and opened training for this role to National Servicemen. However UK based flying schools were unable to cope with the surge in demand so wartime flying schools in Canada and Southern Rhodesia were re-opened to cope.

Trevor decided to re-enlist and was granted a Permanent Commission with back-dated seniority. In 1951 he was once more packing his bags, this time posted as a QFI at No.5 SFTS at Thornhill in Southern Rhodesia, where he instructed student pilots on the Harvard. He remained at Thornhill until 1953 when the Korean armistice was signed, and then returned to the UK.

In 1954 he attended No.231 OCU at RAF Bassingbourn to convert onto the Canberra which, as well as being able to operate as a bomber, was also a very effective reconnaissance aircraft with a service ceiling of around 50,000 feet. Successful completion of OCU saw Trevor joining No.542 Squadron at RAF Wyton, where he continued to fly the aircraft on a variety of operations. On leaving the Squadron two ground appointments followed, the first of these being at the Air Ministry where he became a member of the Air Intelligence Section which, amongst other tasks, used border aerial recce to help analyse potential threats against the West from the Communist East. This was followed by a course at the Staff College.

Trevor returned to operational flying in 1959, this time with a posting to Germany to join No.17 (PR) Squadron at RAF Wildenrath. These were particularly sensitive times during the Cold War with each of the major blocs sensitive to the movements of the other. Many covert operations were carried out by both sides and the use of the

U-2 by the Americans was well publicised when one was shot down over the Soviet Union. However the RAF also played it's part, although these operations have never been publicised, and even today aircrew will not openly discuss them. All Trevor will say is that his Squadron's role was reconnaissance.

The PR Canberra.

In 1961, with completion of his German tour and now a Wing Commander, Trevor returned to the UK when he became the Chief Instructor at No.231 OCU, Bassingbourn, where he had converted onto Canberras some seven years earlier.

By now there was a well established pattern evolving in his career, viz training, reconnaissance and aerial intelligence. It was therefore seemingly a natural progression when, after an appropriate course, in the early 1960's he was posted to MOD producing target materials from US satellite photography and then on to the Central Reconnaissance Establishment at RAF Brampton as the Wing Commander (Operations). The Victor VR2 was now in service as a strategic reconnaissance aircraft and it has been said that it was capable of radar-mapping an area the size of the Mediterranean during a single seven-hour sortie. Today, of course, a satellite could do it in a fraction of the time ! However, as the Wg.Cdr (Ops), Trevor had to be proficient at flying all aircraft which fell within his remit so the Victor was yet another type to enter his log book.

As usual within the RAF, flying duties could be interrupted by administrative tours so it was no surprise for Trevor when his next tour, in August 1973, was to the Supreme Headquarters Allied Powers Europe (SHAPE) HQ at Mons, Belgium, as Intelligence Staff Officer. This was followed by a posting to join a planning team as the Project Officer for a new underground, and nuclear proof, Headquarters at Northwood. The irony of this posting was not lost on Trevor who said, *" It was to be a new HQ for the C in C of the Royal Navy and they were making me the project officer - an RAF pilot !"*

Towards the end of his career he spent a short time, six months, attached to the Air Historical Branch based in London. Here he was tasked with the role of writing 'The History of the Transport Force 1943-1955. *" It was, "* he said, *"an interesting project as I had access to many classified documents including letters from Winston Churchill and the Marshal of the Royal Air Force, Lord Portal."*

Finally, it all came together when Trevor performed his final regular duties as Executive Officer of the Joint Air Reconnaissance Intelligence Centre.

Having been awarded the Air Force Cross (AFC) in Coronation Honours List Wing Commander Trevor Oakey finally retired from the RAF in October 1989, having spent the last ten years in the RAFVR giving Cadets air experience, the last six from Exeter Airport from his new home in Devon. Today he enjoys the comradeship of former aircrew through his membership of the Torbay Branch of The AirCrew Association whilst enjoying retirement in Torquay with his wife, Peggy.

RATS IN THE ROOF - SNAKES ON THE GROUND !

Kenneth T. POLLITT

Ken Pollitt was born in 1923 in the small East Devon village of Aylesbeare, literally within sight of the airfield which was later to become RAF Exeter.   With his brother having joined the RAF in 1938, and witnessing the early activities from the nearby RAF Station, Ken lost little time in leaving his local job as a grocer and presenting himself at the RAF Recruitment Office in Exeter on the 23rd February 1941, his eighteenth birthday.

Events moved quickly and within five weeks he was undergoing assessment at RAF Penarth prior to training as a Flight Mechanic E.   Later, after a four month course at RAF Locking, he was posted to No. 88 Squadron at RAF Attlebridge, Norfolk, to join the maintenance team for their Boston medium-range bombers which were engaged on daylight raids over France.

Towards the end of 1942 he was sent on a Fitter IIE course at Blackpool during which time he volunteered for aircrew as a Flight Engineer, a category in which there was then a shortage. As Ken says, " *I had always wanted to fly and also wanted to become more involved with the action against the enemy.* " His application was accepted, provided he obtained a minimum pass rate of 80% in his Fitter's exam. This achieved, he started Flight Engineer training at RAF St. Athan in March 1943.

Extensive training over the next six weeks saw him covering all mechanical aspects of the US-built 4-engine Liberator, including its engines, airframe, electrics, bomb gear, fuel system and the aircraft's controls. In addition Flight Engineers could, in an emergency, be expected to provide cover as air gunners and Ken was no exception. He successfully completed this aspect of training at RAF Manby gunnery school in Lincolnshire before being posted to Harwell on the next stage to becoming fully-fledged aircrew. Here he joined a crew, led by an Australian pilot - Flying Officer Eric Talbot.

Above: The US built Liberator.
This one was flown by the US Navy from RAF Dunkeswell.

162

Soon after their meeting Ken and his new colleagues were sent to Prestwick where they were briefed that a new Liberator Mk.III had just arrived from the U.S. and they were to fly it to India. None of the gun turrets were operational so their route initially took them over the Atlantic out of range of enemy fighters

Their destination on the first leg was Fez in Morocco although bad weather ultimately led to a diversion to Gibraltar. Weather clearing, their route continued via Fez, across the Sahara to Cairo. From here a further refuelling stop was made at Habbaniya, Iraq, before making final touchdown at Maripore in India where the aircraft was delivered to a Maintenance Unit for modification and equipping for squadron service.

Situated in the Sind Desert with temperatures in excess of 100 degrees F, many airmen at Maripore succumbed to dysentery for which Ken described the cure as *"a dose of castor oil followed by three chalk tablets a day."* However, Ken went a stage further and ended up in the military hospital in Karachi for two weeks ! On recovery he joined his crew for a long train journey, via Calcutta, to Salbani where they joined their new squadron, No. 355.

It was now October 1943 and Ken describes their accommodation as *"poor with rats in the thatched roofs, snakes on the ground and mosquitoes in the air. Furthermore the food was poor, mainly corned beef served in a variety of ways, although when flying on operations we were afforded the luxury of bacon and eggs ! The bright spot was a monthly issue of a bottle of whisky and a bottle of gin although our Irish rear-gunner was subsequently replaced having been found imbibing his ration whilst flying!"*

The squadron was initially equipped with the Mk.III Liberator which carried a crew of seven; pilot, navigator, flight engineer, wireless operator and three gunners. The role of the flight engineer is often under-played but in fact it was a vital element in the aircraft's operation. As mentioned previously, not only was he a stand-by gunner but on many aircraft he fulfilled the role of co-pilot, sitting beside the pilot to operate the throttles and other instruments. Here he recalls another aspect of his role:

" *After the target was bombed and we were away from the target area I would check the bomb bay for any bombs that had hung up and if necessary release them. This involved going into the bomb bay and standing on the catwalk. I would then ask the navigator to open the bomb doors. Then I would manually release the bomb hook. This was not a nice job, the catwalk was only sixteen inches wide and with the bomb doors open it was like standing in space.* "

Ken and his crew completed their full tour of operations which he has described as 'purely routine' although on a flight to bomb Japanese targets at Akyab they lost one of their engines and had to complete their bombing run on only three. However, it was not only the enemy which caused casualties and he recalls administering first-aid when, during an army requested thirteen hour reconnaissance flight to Bentinck Island, a 0.5 mm bullet exploded in the breach of the beam gun and their wireless operator was injured when the bullet casing embedded in his thigh. Ken says this flight was eventful because their Auxiliary Power Unit caught fire as they were coming into land.

However not all such events end happily and Ken has described how on one of their flights the ball gunner reported his intercom was giving trouble. The wireless operator went rearwards to see if he could solve the problem and whilst attempting to do so the turret moved, crushing his chest between the turret and the fuselage floor. Eventually he was released and Ken tended his injured colleague as best he could, injecting morphine to deaden pain. Sadly, on landing he was declared dead.

164

With their operational tour completed on the 19th November 1944, Ken and his crew were posted to Jessore to join No. 292 Squadron, an air sea rescue unit whose task involved searching for missing aircrew and often flying at a height of only fifty feet above the ocean. However, his time with them was short and early in April 1945, after a six week sea voyage, Ken arrived back in the UK.

A period of leave was followed by a posting to No. 466 Squadron, Bomber Command, based at RAF Driffield, Yorks. The war was now ending and the squadron's task was to ferry home troops from India but before doing so most of the crews, who were Australian, returned home.

Ken eventually left the RAF in September 1946 but continued to serve with the RAFVR and the R.Aux.A.F. His latter units were No.3512 'County of Devon' FCU and, after it was disbanded, No. 3 Maritime Unit at RAF Mount Batten, Plymouth. In July 1971 Ken retired after 30 years of regular and reserve RAF service, a fact which was acknowledged by the award of the Air Efficiency Medal

Post war Ken initially joined his brother in a local garage business but later followed a career within the Post Office, eventually retiring as a Postal Executive Officer. Retiring in February 1983, he has never moved far from his roots and today you'll find him happily at home with his wife, Cynthia, in Ottery St. Mary, only a handful of miles from the village where he was born.

LIFE SAVED BY A STALLION !

John E. PRICE.

Johnny Price was born near Glastonbury in August 1920 and attended Wellington School. His parents were farmers and it was natural that on leaving school he would work on the family farm where he developed an instinct for animals which was to stand him in good stead later on.

When war was declared in September 1939 Johnny wasted no time in volunteering for aircrew and enlisted in the RAF before the year ended. Selected for training as a Navigator, he followed the usual process of ITW with later navigation instruction on Anson aircraft before finally attending HCU where he flew on Lancasters and met his new crew prior to joining an operational squadron.

This was No.101 Squadron, Bomber Command, which operated Lancasters and was based at RAF Ludford Magna. It was a lucky tour for Johnny and, after a break, he resumed operations with No.156 Squadron, one of the elite squadrons which operated as Pathfinders flying ahead of the main bomber stream to identify targets.

Until now Johnny's wartime career as a navigator had been more than eventful and, arguably, he was one of Bomber Command's most experienced navigators with forty-two missions over enemy territory behind him, including eleven major raids on Berlin. Indeed the tide of war was slowly turning and the Allies had already established a beachhead in Normandy. It was now the 14th June 1944 and, with all his experience, briefing that night caused Johnny no undue concern when the target was revealed.

166

It was a V-1 site near Lille in Northern France and a mere one hours flight away. Very much routine, their bombing run was successful but as they turned for home everything went tragically wrong. Their Lancaster was hit by a shell from a radar operated gun and severely damaged. Unable to retain control the pilot ordered the crew to bale out. On receipt of the order the Flight Engineer and the Bomb Aimer went ahead of Johnny to jettison the front escape hatch just as the aircraft went into its death throes and violently entered a steep dive. Johnny describes what happened next:

" *When the aircraft fell into a steep dive the manoeuvre was so violent that gravity took over and I was momentarily thrown upwards with such force that my head hit the top of the fuselage. Then, equally fast, I was violently hurled down again. It only took a fraction of a second but the force of the downward thrust catapulted me straight through the escape hatch feet first. Although I didn't realise it at first, it was to save my life. I was the only one who escaped from the already doomed Lancaster..*"

Johnny managed to open his parachute and landed with a thud only to discover that somehow both boots had been ripped from his feet. He knew he was still in occupied France so he instinctively buried his parachute but realised he was unable to walk far. It was also a very dark night so, with his options limited, he settled down as best he could with the intention of surveying his situation at daybreak. As it happened he was discovered by a young French girl shortly after daybreak and he describes the encounter.

" *I think I must have looked a sorry sight for she took pity on me . After seeing I was all right she went away only to reappear shortly afterwards with a plate of eggs, bacon and garlic! It was the first time I'd tasted garlic and I've never forgotten the experience! She then explained that the French Underground in the area had been infiltrated and no longer existed so she thought it was best if I gave myself up to the Germans. I knew it was my duty to evade capture if I could but for a moment I faced a personal dilemma. My older brother, Lawrence, had been a bomber pilot and, incidentally, the squadron commander of the squadron I was now with but, sadly, he had been shot down and killed on the 29th July 1942. If I evaded capture I would be reported as 'missing in action' whereas if I was taken prisoner my family would at least know I was safe. Fortunately the decision was taken out of my hands for the young French girl had already reported my presence to the Germans."*

Johnny was taken into custody and conveyed to the prison in Lille. Now in the custody of the Luftwaffe, he was soon transferred to an interrogation centre in Germany where, taking pity on him and his unshod feet, his captors presented him with a pair of American flying boots. However his ordeal was far from over.

Moved into Eastern Europe, he was incarcerated in a POW camp which was a satellite of Stalag Luft 3. This was the notorious camp at Sagan where earlier fifty British airmen had been brutally murdered after an aborted attempt to escape. This infamous episode was later re-created in the post-war film 'The Great Escape'. Johnny takes up his story:

"Because of that incident further attempts to escape were forbidden by the senior British officers so we just settled down to camp life the best we could . In fact it was bearable thanks to the Red Cross parcels which played a major part in keeping both body and soul together but we didn't realise things were going to get worse. For a start winter was setting in and by clandestine use of a crystal set we heard the Russian army was getting closer."

What happened next was another episode which went down in the annals of WWII history and became known as 'The Long March'. As the Russians drew nearer the Germans decided to move all the prisoners back towards the West and away from the advancing Red Army. Many stories have been written about this marathon trek but here is Johnny's own account.

"It was mid-January 1945 and the weather was harsh and bitterly cold with frequent snow. We were given very little warning to gather any belongings before we started to walk, little knowing at that time that from our camp in Poland the aim was to march us right across Germany, a distance I believe was approximately 800 kms, or 500 miles. It took us about five weeks to make the journey, or at least those of us who did. Sadly, every day took its toll on colleagues who succumbed to the cold and lack of adequate food. I suppose I was lucky to some extent because of my farming background. I knew that, given the freezing night-time temperatures, the warmest spot would be with animals so I made a point of whenever possible to seek them out. I must say that I had some strange bed-fellows including one night sleeping with a great carthorse stallion which just wanted to lie on us! I know one can laugh now but they kept me alive."

In fact Johnny and his fellow survivors did not actually escape the Russians altogether for, reaching Lukenenvalde, they were interned in another camp until they were liberated by the Red Army about three months later. *"Initially the situation was very tense,"* he said. *"We now had Russian guards and there were a number of incidents with our liberators which could easily have flared into something more serious. To make matters worse I developed contagious jaundice and not allowed to eat any fat. It was about this time we discovered there were huge quantities of Red Cross parcels in the camp which the French, who controlled supplies coming into the camp, had been holding on to. Unfortunately there was not much in them that I*

169

could eat.   One day, feeling a little better, I broke out of camp through a hole in the fence to forage for food that I could eat.   I made my way to a small hamlet where there were Russian front-line soldiers in the buildings   I saw some lovely rhubarb growing in the garden.   When I asked the officer if I could have some he tasted a leaf then spat it out, telling me to get some bread from the cooks in the square.

The next day I was told there was some sugar at a farm in a different direction so I made my way there and managed to fill a bag with as much as I could carry.   I was walking back along the cobbled street with an American colleague, who'd also been after some sugar, when I heard a bicycle bell ringing.   The rider was the Russian Commandant of the local town who rode straight at us and, when he buckled his wheel, he drew his gun and was ready to shoot us.   He was blind drunk but fortunately had an interpreter with him who defused the situation.   At least now I had the right food.

Fortunately a little later we learned that the Americans were 'just up the road' so we high-tailed it towards them as fast as we could.   The difference in treatment was remarkable and within a very short period I was flown to Brussels on the first leg of my journey home."

Johnny left the RAF in January 1946 and returned to life as a farmer.   He has also managed to maintain links with France where over sixty years ago his flying career came to an abrupt end.

Today he enjoys a quiet retirement with his wife, Joanne, at Exmouth.

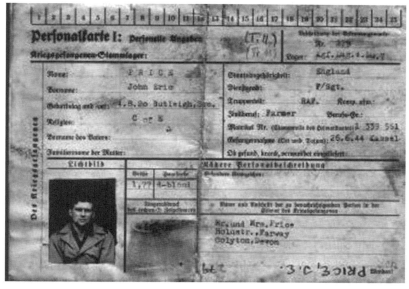

Johnny Price's only souvenir of his RAF service is his POW Camp ID Card,
pictured above with an enlarged photograph - 1944.

ALL HE SAW WAS MILES OF WATER !

HAROLD REVILL

Harold was born in the Lancashire town of Standish in May 1923 and later educated at St.Peter's School in York. It was whilst there that a visiting RAF recruitment team recommended him for a 'University Short Course'. He subsequently arrived at Glasgow University in February 1941 where he was enrolled in the University Air Squadron and undertook the aircrew ITW course whilst simultaneously studying 1st year engineering. Then, in September 1941, Harold undertook 'grading' at RAF Booker where, after six hours flying in a Tiger Moth, he was selected for further training as a pilot. Two months later he arrived in the United States and was posted to the U.S. Naval Reserve base at Grosse Isle, Michigan, where primary flying training for pilots was on the Stearman bi-plane. With the first stage completed, he next travelled the length of the United States for the second phase.

This was at the US Naval base at Pensacola in Florida between January and July 1942. Here instruction was on a wide range of training aircraft, including the Vultee Valiant and its 'look alike', the North American Harvard. However, being a navy base, experience on flying boats followed, initially being on the Vought Kingfisher and, later, the Consolidated Catalina. When the course was completed he was awarded his pilot's wings and headed north again, this time to Canada. His destination was the RCAF base at Charlottetown on Prince Edward Island where, before commencing a four month course on General Reconnaissance, he learned he had been awarded a commission. Flying the Avro Anson, the course was a prelude to returning to the UK to attend OTU at RAF Alness, on the Cromaty Firth. Arriving there in January 1943, Harold once more found himself flying Catalinas.

Although in theory one's time at OTU was training for operational duties, in practice it could be much different. Harold was to spend the next five months 'on the job' training with operational sorties over the North Atlantic. Their role during this period was two-fold, namely providing escort for our convoys and also undertaking vital anti-submarine patrols.

Above: Harold, aged 82 years, and a Catalina flying boat he flew on patrol sixty-two years earlier. The aircraft's s exceptional endurance and long range made it an ideal aircraft for lengthy ocean patrols.

Completion of his course in Scotland saw Harold on the move again, this time to join No.212 Squadron which operated Catalinas in the Far East and was part of South East Asia Air Command. Frequently moving, they operated from Korangi Creek, on the edge of the Sind Desert near Karachi, Cochin on the West coast of India and Koggala Lake on the southern tip of Ceylon. The drill was always the same, long, lonely patrols over the Indian Ocean, keeping a watching brief over our convoys whilst at the same time searching for the slightest sign of enemy submarine activity. He was once asked to sum up his wartime experiences and philosophically replied,

173

" That either calls for a book or nothing. There is so very much, or when one looks at the experiences of some people, so many far greater than mine, there is so very little. I can say this. We were out typically for twenty-one hours at a time and we saw lots and lots of water. I like to think that we saved many lives. "

The fact that the presence of a patrolling Catalina seriously inhibited the actions of U-boat commanders is not in doubt. To Harold those long hours of patrol over endless stretches of water must have seemed like an eternity. Yet, paradoxically, he did save lives although how many will never be known.

Harold left the RAF in September 1946 and returned to Canada where initially he was employed in the design office of AV Roe. However at the outbreak of the Korean War, and the announcement there was a shortage of flying instructors, Harold joined the RCAF and became an instructor training the influx of new pilots from Canada, Britain and some of the NATO countries. When the war ended he remained in the RCAF and moved to the Institute of Aviation Medicine in Toronto where he became involved in research work.

Eventually leaving the Service, he became what he describes as a 'bush pilot' but was actually ferrying supplies for the construction of the 'mid-Canada Line', a defensive radar chain. This sometimes meant flying a Catalina between the lakes of Canada's Northern Territory but also the DC-4, Beaver and Otter on other occasions. However by 1969 he decided upon a complete career change and enrolled at the University of British Columbia to study law after which he became a successful lawyer.

He returned to the UK in 1997 and now lives in Topsham.

HE WENT 'GARDENING' ALONG THE FRENCH COAST !

Gerald ROGERS.

Gerry Rogers was born at Ladock in Cornwall on the 26th September 1920 and educated locally at St. Austell.   On leaving school he joined WH Smith (Wholesale), working within the distribution side of the company.   He was still eighteen when war was declared on 3rd September 1939, an event which saw him immediately volunteering for aircrew. Although accepted for 'Direct Entry Aircrew' it was actually August 1940 before he was called into service.

Selected for training in the dual role of Wireless Operator/Air Gunner, Gerry under took basic morse code training in Blackpool, where he says he reached 8 words per minute, before advancing to the RAF's No.2 Signals School at Yatesbury for more intensive training. This was followed by gunnery training at Jurby on the Isle of Man after which, with all training complete, he was posted to RAF Chivenor, North Devon, which operated an OTU for the Bristol Beaufort, a twin-engine torpedo bomber.   With a crew of four, it was here that Gerry teamed up with the other three members of the crew prior to progressing to active squadron duty.

For Gerry a squadron posting meant returning home to his native Cornwall, to St. Eval where he joined No.22 Squadron of Coastal Command.   Whilst here Gerry and his crew undertook a wide variety of roles, one of which was 'gardening', as he now explains:

" *One of our greatest menaces   at that time was the German U-boat which was capable of inflicting   heavy losses on our convoys which were carrying vital supplies.   One solution was convoy surveillance, keeping a diligent watch for any*

hostile craft, but there was another.   That was to try and prevent   the U-boats
operating in the first place   and that was one of our roles.   Flying alternate nights,
under the cover of darkness we would lay mines in the shipping lanes off the French
coast in the hope that they would hinder the operation of enemy submarines and
surface craft within our waters.   Known as 'gardening' we flew many such ops and
although we always returned unscathed there were   always intense moments when
shore batteries opened up and there was always the threat of enemy night-fighters."

Gerry Rogers. second from left, with other crew members
of his Beaufort torpedo bomber.

After six months of 'gardening' from his Cornish cliff-top base, Gerry, together with
the rest of the Squadron, was posted to the Middle East where he says they were based
in the middle of nowhere in the desert at a spot identified only as 'Landing Ground 86'.
Much of their work was ferrying with some excitement when they encountered the
Italian Fleet between Malta and Libya where it was guarding Rommel's supply line
to the Afrika Corps.

However as events in the Mediterranean were turning in the Allies' favour, their stay was relatively short as Gerry explains:

"We were only in the Middle East for six months when we were suddenly sent to Ceylon. In fact it was like a peace time service as the nearest 'Jap' was in Singapore and well out of the range of our aircraft. I suppose that also had some bearing on the fact I wasn't there very long either and in late 1943 I was on my way home again."

The Bristol Beaufort flown by No.22 Squadron at RAF St. Eval.

On his return Gerry found himself in the role of signals instructor at Squires Gate, Blackpool. Now flying in Ansons, his role was to teach new wireless operators the mechanics of operating their equipment in the air. The posting lasted eight months and then he was off again, this time to return to operational flying with a new squadron and a fresh aircraft, the Catalina.

This new posting was to No.202 Squadron which operated North Atlantic patrols from Castle Archdale in Northern Ireland. Made by 'Consolidated' in the US, the Catalina had the benefit of exceptionally long endurance which made it ideal for protecting our convoys far out into the Atlantic Gerry says that patrols of sixteen to twenty hours were common and although they rarely had any sightings of an enemy this was, in itself, a positive factor for it meant their surveillance were keeping our convoys, and men, safe.

When war ended Gerry returned to the Signals School at Yatesbury where he had originally trained only now he was a Warrant Officer. Given a role as 'Assistant' to the Station W.O, he remained there until demobilised in the Autumn of 1946. Once asked to sum up his wartime experience he replied,

"Obviously flying on ops there were a few exciting moments, including one with a couple of Messerschmitts, but we always came through unscathed. and I honestly believe someone was looking after me every time we took off. That said, I suppose our role was always going to be largely overshadowed by the heroic deeds of Bomber Command but each, in their own way, were equally vital. "

On leaving the RAF Gerry returned to his old employer, WH Smith (Wholesale), finally retiring in 1981 after 47 years service as head of their West of England Group . Today, recently a widower, he lives in retirement in Plymouth where he is active as the Social Secretary of the Plymouth Branch of the ACA

In April 2005 he returned to RAF Chivenor where over sixty years before he had been introduced to the Beaufort and which today, by coincidence, is also the home of 'A' Flight, No.22 Squadron, the squadron he first joined in 1942. The only difference is today they undertake a 'Search & Rescue' role with Sea King helicopters.

178

HE BROUGHT THE KING's SPEECH TO THE NAVY !

Stacey F. SIMKINS

Born in London in April 1924, Stacey Simkins worked as a Clerk in London on leaving school and joined the Auxiliary Fire Service as a messenger, later as a fireman, but as soon as he was able volunteered to join the RAF as aircrew. As a result he was called up shortly before his nineteenth birthday, in March 1943, when he was assessed for further training as a wireless operator / air gunner (WOP/AG).

Stacey progressed through the normal training process with flying experience at Yatesbury on the De Havilland Rapide and Proctor aircraft, followed by Air Gunner School at Castle Kennedy before undertaking crew training at OTU, Enstone, where he crewed a Wellington. This was followed by HCU's at Topcliffe and Wombleton on the 4-engine Halifax prior to joining Bomber Command and No.102 Squadron based at RAF Pocklington.

Asked about memorable moments, with typical cockney humour he chose to highlight the funnier moments of his wartime flying career, both in the air and on the ground. Despite flying a number of 'ops' against heavily defended targets in the Ruhr and Northern France when asked about any problems he replied, *"Only with our pilot !"*

He then went on to relate how, on returning from a raid on an oil refinery in the Ruhr, their pilot, who needed corrective vision, had sat on his glasses ... and broken them! *"As a result"*, he said, *"we landed at the wrong end of the runway and when he realised his mistake he panicked with the result that we ended up about three fields away. It could have been worse but another aircraft had previously gone through the boundary fence and we just went through the gap ! Then on another occasion he came in to land on a main road which ran parallel to the runway. Fortunately he realised his mistake and aborted the landing just in time. We never saw him after that!*

Asked about any damage they may have sustained whilst on operations, he replied, *"Not a sausage. The nearest I ever came to it was once when, as the wireless operator, I picked up an unidentified blip on my screen which could have been an enemy night-fighter. Anyway neither of our gunners saw anything and it seems the 'blip' passed beneath us. "*

Stacey however has many 'memorable moments' which show how aircrew were able to relax even though risking their lives on an almost daily basis. Amongst these tales was how he and his Flight Engineer pal, Ken Tyrrell, used to go into town and order one portion of 'pie and chips' with two knives and forks and split the meal down the middle. An interesting tale in itself but even more so when Stacey explains that his crew mate was *the* Ken Tyrrell who went on to found the famous Formula One racing team !

For many servicemen the 6th June, 1944, occupies a special spot in their memories and for Stacey it was no different. However his recollections are not quite what one expects and come with that blend of unique cockney humour. Here's an account in his own words.

"It was the night of 5th/6th June 1944 and we took-off in a Wimpey (an affectionate term for the Wellington bomber) from Enstone. loaded with 'window' (thin metallic strips which when dropped confused enemy radar). We flew over the North Sea, back and forth, stuffing it down the flare chute. On return we diverted to Moreton in Marsh owing to fog and crashed aircraft at our base. We landed OK. We were picked up by the crew van to return, very slowly, and on the way back we had an argument with a Sherman tank. We lost!

A close-up showing the nose of a Wellington bomber.

Had June 6th off so four of us hitched a lift to Oxford where, shortly after arrival, we were accosted by two WRENS who shanghaied us to a dance . At five minutes to nine the band stops and the WRENS C.O., a Lt. Cdr., announces the King is to make a speech as it was D-day and produces a radio. Anyway, the wireless didn't work and the C.O. asks for a volunteer to mend it. As the only W/Op there I had no option but to volunteer although I was absolutely clueless about civvy radios. Anyway I took the back off the set and luckily spotted a loose wire and, even better a spare blob of solder. I touched the wire to the solder and, hooray, it works ! As I had to keep the two bits in contact they provided me with an empty upturned fire bucket to sit on.

I sat there throughout the National Anthem, the King's speech and then the National Anthem again. I thought that I must be the only serviceman who's sat through two National Anthems in the presence of a senior officer without getting his b***s chewed off! Afterwards the four of us were invited back stage to sample copious draughts of 'neaters' None of us remembered the journey back to camp although I do recall that this was in a R.N. staff car."

As the war in Europe ended Stacey and the rest of his crew were selected for the planned 'Tiger Force' assault against the Japanese. Fortunately the dropping of atomic bombs on Hiroshima and Nagasaki brought the war to an end and they were not required. As Stacey said, *"When they heard the magnificent seven were coming, they quit !"* In March, 1947, Stacey returned to civvy street. where his cheery cockney character helped him to carve a career in the Import / Export business, becoming a Director of his company.

He finally retired in June 1986 and moved to Devon four months later. Today he and his wife, Gwen, enjoy life in peaceful Dawlish.

There is a more serious side to Stacey and amongst his pursuits he enjoys writing poetry. He once wrote the following lines in memory of his fallen colleagues.

> *"They died that we might live,*
> *Gave all they had to give.*
> *I know my pals are dead*
> *But they live still, in my head.*

HE CARRIES HIS WAR SOUVENIR AT ALL TIMES !

Cyril A. SMITH MBE.

Cyril was born at Brocklesby, North Lincolnshire, in February 1923 and educated at Brigg Grammar School from which he obtained temporary employment as a bank clerk whilst waiting to join the RAF at the age of eighteen.   Having volunteered for aircrew he was selected for training as an Observer following eye problems whilst at ITW at Newquay. His practical training was on Ansons at Staverton and Moreton Valence.

Operational training continued at No.10 OTU, Abingdon, where the aircraft flown was the Whitley. This included a short detachment to Coastal Command at St. Eval where the Whitley was flown operationally on convoy escort duties and anti-submarine patrols. Despite flying eight sorties whilst at the Cornish base, plus two decoy operations to France from Abingdon, Cyril's ultimate destiny was not with Coastal Command but with heavy bombers.   This saw him being posted to the Heavy Conversion Unit at Ricall, Yorkshire, where he and his new crew trained together on the Halifax Mk I Then, after training was successfully completed, Cyril and his crew were posted to No.51 Squadron which operated the Halifax MkII from their base at Snaith in Yorkshire.   Later, to facilitate the expansion of Bomber Command, 'C' Flight of No.51 Squadron was split off to form the nucleus of No.578 Squadron, also based at Snaith.   This new Squadron flew its first mission on the night of the 20th January 1944 when two of its aircraft were borrowed from neighbouring 51 Squadron. One of these was Cyril's. Their target was Berlin.   Cyril, who had already completed four raids on Berlin was now scheduled to make his fifth trip. However, this time things went drastically wrong as he now explains:

" Initially we were only a stand-by crew as our own aircraft was u/s and our Flight Engineer had been taken ill with appendicitis.   However we were allocated a brand new aircraft together with a Flight Engineer making his first 'op'. Everything went well at first.   We were on track and time and I was sat at my navigator's desk plotting our course as we headed across Northern Germany.   Then, suddenly, all hell broke loose as we were attacked by a JU-88 night-fighter which opened fire on us with its cannon.   One of the shells unfortunately exploded under my navigator's table and I instantly knew I'd been hit.   The aircraft was badly damaged and the skipper realised we had no chance of continuing to our target. Taking evasive action, we jettisoned our bomb load somewhere over the Kiel Canal and somehow I managed to plot a course towards home on a track which took us over Heligoland and across the North Sea.   We were lucky and eventually made it home.   However, I understand the Engineering Officer was a bit dismayed at the damage to a brand new aircraft !"

On landing it was discovered that   Cyril had received a serious leg injury with fragments of cannon shell penetrating deep into his flesh and tibia. This initially meant a stay of four weeks in York Military Hospital followed by an enforced rest at the RAF Rehabilitation Unit in Loughborough. However, his injuries had perhaps been a blessing in disguise. He explains why.

"Whilst I was recuperating the rest of my crew, with a new navigator, continued on

184

ops. Sadly on one of their raids over Germany, target Stuttgart, they were badly shot up and their Halifax severely damaged. They managed to cross the Channel on the homeward leg but the aircraft's fuel tanks were leaking and, although they almost made base, the aircraft was too crippled and crashed. Only the Navigator and the Flight Engineer managed to escape and the rest of the crew, my friends, were killed."

Returning from convalescence, on the 6th June 1944 Cyril joined No.578 Squadron which had been partially formed from aircraft from 'C' Flight of his old Squadron and was now based at Burn in Yorkshire. He was found a position in their new office until the end of the year and, although strictly not allowed to fly, occasionally found himself called for duty as a stand-in navigator when the necessity arose. However his injuries continued to plague him and he was eventually invalided out of the service. In fact to this day he has the discomfort of still having pieces of cannon shell lodged in his leg. However he has a happier reminder of service life and, despite his injuries, 1944 was not entirely a bad year. Two years earlier, whilst at ITW in Newquay, Cyril had met Megan and in 1944 they had a service wedding.

Post war Cyril became an HM. Inspector of Taxes and was transferred to Torquay in 1962. Awarded the MBE in 1986 he replied, *" They said it was for 'Services to the Community' but I hardly think it was for being a Tax Inspector. It was more likely to be for cricket. My injuries prevented me from playing but I was a local umpire for many years in both Devon and Cornwall."*

A member of the Torbay branch of the AirCrew Association, whilst not enjoying the best of health, today Cyril is peacefully retired in Torquay with Megan, his wife for more than sixty years.

SOLO AGAIN AFTER FIFTY YEARS !

Alfred D.G. WALLEN, MBE

Alf Wallen was born, bred and educated within the City of Exeter. Volunteering for aircrew, he joined the RAFVR on 7th August 1941 whilst still only seventeen although a year was to pass before he was told to report to the Aircrew Reception Centre (ACRC) at Lords Cricket Ground. After ITW in Torquay he was posted to No.21 EFTS at RAF Booker for 'Grading' which entailed some twelve hours flying on Tiger Moths to determine one's aptitude for pilot training.

Initially Alf's worst fears were realised when he arrived at Heaton Park, Manchester, a transit station. Awaiting an overseas posting for flying training, he was told it was to be as a navigator. However, a week later, his luck changed with the news that he was to undertake pilot training after all. As a result, in early July 1943, he duly arrived at the United States Navy Air Station at Grosse Ile in Michigan for training by the US navy. Alf takes up his story from there:

" After eleven hours dual instruction on a Stearman I made my first solo flight and seemed to be making satisfactory progress. Things changed, however, after about thirty hours or so when I started S' turns and sideslips to land in a circle. Remember this was a course for US Navy pilots who eventually would be required to land on a Carrier. To me these circles appeared to have a diameter not much greater than the wing span of a Stearman but they were probably a little larger than that. In order to pass this stage one had to land in the circle at least three times out of six attempts. Unfortunately my maximum was only two and I suspect those were more by luck than judgement. However, that was the end of my pilot training."

Luckily, it was not the end of Alf's flying for he was sent to Canada to await a vacancy on a navigators' course. This came early in 1943 at No.1 Central Navigation School, Rivers, Manitoba. He graduated on the 5th May 1944, was commissioned as a Pilot Officer and subsequently arrived back in the UK a few days before D-day.

However for the remainder of the year he was on further training and conversion courses, starting in early July at No10 (Operational) AFU, with instruction on Ansons before moving on to No.84 OTU at RAF Desborough where flying was on Wellingtons. The final stage came when he moved to No.1668 Heavy Conversion Unit (HCU) at Bottesford where he met his new crew and converted onto the Lancaster preparatory to joining his first squadron. Training over, Alf explains what happened next.

"We were given the option of moving onto one of the Pathfinder Squadrons but my skipper, a much older and wiser bird than me, opted for a normal squadron 'to learn our trade'. In the event, we were not posted directly to a squadron but to RAF Feltwell on a Gee-H course, the equipment being the latest 'state of the art' navigational aid. With our newly acquired knowledge we were then posted directly to No.514 Squadron which operated Lancasters from RAF Waterbeach in Cambridgeshire and where, although only a sprog crew, we could be used as Gee-H leaders if necessary.

Our first 'op'. came on the 26th February, 1945 - target Dortmund. Other targets seemed to quickly follow and although the war in Europe was reaching its closing stages, we still had considerable enemy defences to penetrate on occasions.. Although we were hit by shrapnel a few times the engines kept working and we didn't suffer any injuries which was the main thing. I suppose you could say we were lucky!"

Left: Alf Wallen in 1944.
Below: The York, a type he flew on the fast route between the UK and India.

With the last few weeks of war came 'Operation Manna', the dropping of essential food and other supplies to the starving people of Holland.   Alf was about half way through his first tour when they were deployed to take part and on the 29th April 1945 he made his first 'Manna' drop on The Hague. This was followed by two more 'Manna' flights on the 1st and 3rd May, the last basically ending his wartime operations.   During the next two months the squadron was engaged in repatriating Belgian refugees and bringing back POWs from Belgium, France and Italy.

One interesting fact Alf mentioned was that by way of a 'thank-you' to their ground crews, who had so efficiently repaired and serviced the aircraft during the bombing campaign, when the war was over they took them on aerial tours of the Ruhr area to show them the devastation their bombers had caused.

At the end of July 1945 Alf was hurriedly posted from Bomber Command to Transport Command, initially with a view to ferrying extra troops to the Far East. He sums up his feelings at the time with the following comment .

"I was not too sorry when the atom bombs were dropped on Hiroshima and Nagasaki and forced the Japanese into surrender."

He was to spend the rest of his time in Transport Command when, after a conversion course, he joined No.246 Squadron which was equipped with York aircraft and flew the fast freight routes from the UK to India. Now a Flt.Lt., Alf was granted an Extended Service Commission in June 1946 but in the December opted to take his 'A' class release.

On settling into civilian life he soon decided an office environment was not for him so in August 1950, shortly before his 26th birthday, he joined the former Exeter City Police which later was amalgamated into the Devon & Cornwall Constabulary. In an eventful career, he served as a Detective Inspector with the Regional Crime Squad and later became deputy head of the Force CID.

Other senior appointments followed, including a secondment to the Office of H.M. Inspectorate of Constabulary, a post which saw him visiting Hong Kong on three occasions when problems arose within the colonial force. Awarded the MBE in June 1982, he was appointed Chief Officer of the Island Police in Guernsey. He retired at the expiry of his contract but held other positions on the Island until March 1995. He was a member of the Guernsey Flying Club and fifty years after his first solo flight in the United States he flew solo again, this time in a Cessna.

Today, Alf lives in Budleigh Salterton with his wife, Pauline, and continues to enjoy a number of leisure activities.

189

THE JAPS GUARDED OUR FUEL DUMP !

Norman William WALTER.

Born and educated in Plymouth, Norman Walter had an early baptism of the horrors of war for he was only sixteen when his home was bombed during the 1941 raids on the city. Sadly, the following year, his brother, Arthur, was killed aboard the cruiser HMS Nigeria, then engaged on the Malta convoys. Such tragedies, however, only made Norman more resolved to play his part and to volunteer for aircrew. In 1942 he took the first steps by becoming an Air Cadet. Weekends were spent at RAF Mount Batten with No.10 Sunderland Squadron RAAF, where Australian instructors provided training in gunnery, navigation, and other subjects relevant for potential aircrew.

This experience stood him in good stead when, in December 1943, he was able to enlist at a time when fewer aircrew were being recruited. Accepted for training as an Air Gunner, he started ground training at No. 4 Elementary Gunnery School, RAF Bridgnorth, and then flying training in Ansons at the Air Gunnery School, RAF Bedlington. Norman described their pilots as *'battle hardened Poles who were on a 'rest cure'. They smiled at we poor pale-faced cadets as they threw the aircraft around as though it was a fighter!"* Further flying experience at RAF Chipping Warden was on Wellingtons which he describes as *'being clapped out and always smelling of oil and fuel leaks which was not very confidence building.'*

Posting to No. 1657 Heavy Conversion Unit (HCU) at RAF Stradishall followed and an introduction to the Stirling heavy bomber. Norman was not impressed, saying the aircraft had been designed in a hurry, was greatly under-powered and had an inherently fragile undercarriage which was prone to collapse on landing. Add other problems and he was thankful when, at the end of the course, he was switched to the far superior and much loved Lancaster where he and his colleagues finally gelled together as 'a crew'.

190

In January 1945 they joined No. 622 Squadron at RAF Mildenhall, to fly Lancasters. With the war now in its final stages Norman's operational experience was mainly to targets in Germany when they were usually well escorted by Spitfire and Mustang fighters. As a result he says their losses were few and in sharp contrast to earlier days when between forty to sixty aircraft could be lost on a major raid. However losses did still occur and Norman recalls two raids his crew made on Cologne.

" This surprised our crew as, looking down, the city appeared already quite devastated. It was in ruins and its two large bridges were broken in the river. Nevertheless the German anti-aircraft fire was still deadly and on our second raid a Lancaster from our sister squadron was flying quite close to us. Suddenly there was a loud bang and the aircraft had received a direct hit. One wing was blown off and it fell to the ground with no survivors. Its crew included a close friend of mine who had been in training with me from day one. Years later I ascertained that he was buried in Northern France. "

In 1945, during the final months of the war, the squadron joined others in undertaking humanitarian flights known as 'Operation Manna'.   These comprised dropping essential food and other supplies to the starving people of Holland. Norman says they were exciting trips as they had to fly very low and the Dutch people would stand on the roofs and wave like mad whilst the farmers marked out their fields - 'Thank You RAF'.

At much the same time the squadron also undertook the rewarding role of transporting former British POWs home, many having been incarcerated since Dunkirk.   On each flight up to twenty-six of them would cram into the Lancaster, but they didn't mind the discomfort, they were going home!

191

RAF Mildenhall - January 1945.
Norman, far right, with the rest
of his crew beneath the nose
of their Lancaster bomber of
No.622 Squadron.

At the end of the war Norman received a commission but there was little need for air gunners and he was switched to administrative duties. It was now January 1946 and he found himself flying to the Far East aboard a brand new York aircraft bound for Singapore. *"It was quite an eventful flight "*, he says. *"We seemed to stay overnight at each of the five transit stations with engine faults on our new aircraft. This included eight days at Karachi in a huge transit tented camp at Mauripur with thousands of servicemen awaiting repatriation back to the UK. Locally, the mood for independence was strong and if we visited the city we were likely to be stoned or spat upon by locals shouting 'Ja Hind' or ' Brits go Home' - not a very nice experience. Reaching Singapore I passed a few days in a transit dormitory at the back of the Raffles Hotel, with rope beds and many cockroaches ! "*

Norman's ultimate destination was No. 3 Far East Staging Post at Don Muang, Bangkok's main airport through which hundreds of RAF Transport movements were made each week. He says, "*The RAF Station at the airport had many surprises, the main one being the large bulk fuel storage in the middle of the airfield, mainly in 40 gallon drums. These were, of course attractive for many of the local robbers. The solution was to have them guarded by hundreds of Japanese military prisoners awaiting repatriation. These had set up their own authorised camp and were armed with large sticks and ferocious dogs, but they certainly stopped the large scale pilfering of fuel. When acting as Duty Officer I would make twice nightly visits to the fuel dump and found the Japanese to be very subservient with few speaking English but my biggest worry was that there were lots of snakes around.*"

After ten months at Bangkok Norman was posted to Ceylon, now Sri Lanka, as a Movements Officer with No.205 Squadron which operated Sunderlands from RAF Koggala. It was an interesting period because the aircraft were authorised to carry fare-paying passengers, mainly businessmen, to Penang and Singapore as an early effort to reconstruct trade links in the aftermath of the war. However, the arrival of civil aircraft ended this role for the versatile Sunderland, gradually making them redundant. Norman was posted back to Singapore when he says, " *nine of the aircraft had just been dumped in the jungle. It was a very sad sight.*"

In April 1948 Norman returned to the UK for demobilisation and, with no firm plans, in the August joined the Exeter City Police Force. Successfully completing his two year probationary service, he decided it was not the career he sought. In January 1950 he re-enlisted in the RAF as an Equipment and Movements Officer and was later awarded a Permanent Commission. His first posting after re-training was to RAF Exeter which serviced South Devon's two ground fighter control radar installations at RAF Exminster and RAF Hope Cove. However, he particularly recalls a tragic accident which occurred during his stay. "*It was a Friday afternoon,*" he said. "*Our unit was closing down for the weekend when a visiting Canberra came in to drop off*

193

a passenger, a serving RAF officer. The pilot did not stop the engines and took off almost immediately, only to fly into a flock of birds. Both engines cut and the aircraft crashed into a field near what was then the Black Horse Transport Cafe. Both crew died immediately."

After two years at Exeter, many postings followed. These included RAF Luqa in Malta from where he returned to the Far East where experienced Movements Officers were urgently required. Returning home in 1956, he was posted to RAF St. Mawgan just in time to see the phasing out of the last Coastal Command Lancasters. Other postings were to Gibraltar and later, in January 1967, to Aden with the task of evacuating all British military personnel by the end of the year. Terrorist activity was prevalent and during his stay three soldiers were shot by insurgents on the far side of the airfield.

Between 1972 and 1975 he was in Malta again, returning to the UK for his final posting. This was to No. 25 MU at RAF Hartlebury which he describes as '*the saddest of his career*'. Now a Squadron Leader, he was appointed 'team leader' to oversee its closure with the redundancy of 240 civilian staff. It was closed on schedule in November 1976, when he decided to retire.

Retirement however did not mean the end of Norman's work in aviation. His vast experience in aircraft movements and equipment saw him gain a five year contract to work in Saudi Arabia with the Royal Saudi Air Force which was followed by another five year contract with the Sultan of Oman's Government and promotion to become Secretary to the Tender Board for all Military Supplies.

Travelling days now over, today Norman and his wife, Margaret, enjoy a peaceful retirement in the Exeter suburb of Pinhoe.

194

MORE PROMPT THAN THE TRAINS !

John J. WARREN

John was born at Bridgend, South Wales, in the Summer of 1937 so, not surprisingly is known to his many friends as 'Taff'.   On finishing education at the local Technical College he enlisted in the RAF at the age of eighteen as a Radar Mechanic / Fitter and after training at No.2 Radar School, RAF Yatesbury, served at a number of RAF Stations. These included Pembroke Dock, St. Mawgan, Mountbatten and, finally, at No.4 Joint Services Trials Unit which was constructing Blue Steel guided missiles for ultimate service with the V-Bomber Force.

However a complete change in John's career came in 1961 when he was accepted for NCO pilot training.   This was initially carried out on Jet Provost Mk III aircraft at No.3 FTS, RAF Leeming before continuing with advanced flying at No.5 FTS, RAF Oakington. Here he flew the Vampire T11 and the Varsity.   He was awarded his pilot's wings on 6th September 1963 and three weeks later married his childhood sweetheart, Anne.

John's first posting as a newly qualified pilot saw him remaining in Flying Training Command with a two and a half year tour as a Staff Pilot on Varsity aircraft based at RAF Topcliffe and used for training Air Electronics Officers (AEOs) and Signallers. When the tour ended he undertook an officers' training course at RAF Henlow following which he was commissioned and posted to join RAF Transport Command as 'Specialist Aircrew'.

This was a term used to denote those whose service career would be limited in respect of promotion but in return they would be engaged fully on flying duties and not subject to 'ground tours' which officers seeking high rank had to undertake. His initial posting in his new category was to RAF Lyneham, where he joined No.511 Squadron, and later at RAF Brize Norton when the Squadron relocated there in 1969. Flying the Bristol Britannia, first as co-pilot and then as Captain, this began a seven year spell when he literally 'flew the world' with log book entries showing destinations not only throughout Europe but also in the US and the Far East.

Asked about any memorable incidents during this period, he replied:

" Mostly it was fairly routine, carrying troops here and there and also supplies to our overseas bases which were still quite considerable at that time. However one incident which does come to mind really started in 1971 when the situation on the India sub-continent deteriorated. In March civil war erupted in East Pakistan, followed by border disputes with India which culminated with the outbreak of war between the two countries in early December. Eventually, when peace ensued, there was the division of Pakistan into two separate countries, East & West Pakistan, the former becoming known as Bangladesh. Ultimately there was a great refugee problem which was exacerbated by a large degree of enforced repatriation on both sides. The United Nations were brought in to assist in a humanitarian role and

196

that's where the RAF came in. Working under the auspices of the UN, in 1973 'Operation Lucan' was set up and our role was to transport refugees from Dacca in the East to Karachi in the West and vice-versa. Each leg entailed a flight of over 1500 miles across India and we would do a return trip a day I suppose seeing the plight of refugees is something which always remains in your mind."

Above is a Bristol Britannia in flight whilst the photograph of John used as a caption is of him in the Captain's seat during 'Operation Lucan'.

John left Brize Norton in early 1974 and in the June returned to RAF Lyneham to join No.216 Squadron which operated the Comet Mk.IVc. However a year after his arrival the Squadron was axed in defence cuts and he found himself posted to RAF Finningley in September 1975.

This was a return to Flying Training Command for Finningley operated as a Flying Training School for Navigators, AEO's and Flight Engineers. John's duties as a Staff Pilot were to fly the trainees for the practical aspects of their course. The aircraft used for this purpose was the Dominie, the military version of the twin jet HS125.

The Dominie

His tour at Finningley ended when, in January 1979, he returned to RAF Brize Norton to join Transport Command's No.10 Squadron. However there had been changes since he was last there, notably the phasing in of the Tristar and VC-10K in air-refuelling roles. John was to fly the versatile VC-10 and, once again, progressed from co-pilot to Captain. He was to remain there for the next nine years, a period which once more saw him flying to destinations around the world. Again asked about any highlights, he replied:

"Whilst to us it was all pretty much routine, I suppose each flight was different in some way. We saw a lot of the world and some flights were more memorable than others. We also met a number of interesting people and I flew a number of VIPs over the years. These included Margaret Thatcher whilst she was Prime Minister. She was a delightful person to fly and was always careful to see the crew were looked after. On one occasion I flew her to a G8 Conference at Cancun in Mexico after which we took her to Mexico City for another meeting. Whilst there the city was rocked by a serious earthquake and the fact she was there at the time made all the

news headlines. *Interestingly, her main concern was for us and she went out of her way to make sure we were all safe. We were and so was the aircraft which was just as well as, part of her busy schedule, we flew her to another conference in Bermuda on the way home. I also flew the Duke of Edinburgh to Saudi Arabia when he represented Britain at the funeral of a member of the Saudi Royal family.*

However I suppose in some way the flights which stick most in my mind were those I flew during the Falkland's War. Our staging route was Brize Norton, Dakar in West Africa, and then Ascension. Everything for the Falklands went out of Ascension, a small volcanic outcrop in the middle of the South Atlantic. Our flights were mainly troop and supply movements but there were also those which highlighted the casualties of war . Seriously wounded troops, after life-saving surgery on the Islands, would be transferred by HMS Heclar, a Hospital Ship, to the nearest friendly country to await repatriation home. This was to Montevideo in Uruguay and that's where we came in. Flying a specially equipped VC-10, marked with the Red Cross, we would repatriate them from Montevideo and fly them home. On such flights we carried a full surgical team and the journey home was in two stages, firstly from Uruguay to Ascension and from there direct to Brize Norton. Seeing our passengers we could not help feeling a great sadness for many were severely burned, some being survivors from the Sir Galahad."

It was around this time that John and his crew received a mention in the John Junor column of the Sunday Express dated March 6 1983. It is perhaps worth quoting here.

< The Schedule said that we would leave Port Stanley airport at 8am and arrive at Brize Norton, 8000 miles away at noon the next day. We arrived in Ascension in a Hercules precisely on schedule. We landed in Dakar in thick fog. Again on the dot. And Brize Norton ?   I was on the flight deck of the VC10 with Flight Lieutenants 'Taff' Warren and Mike Grey as we landed and taxied to the terminal

building.   When the engines were switched off it was not 11.59.   Nor was it 12.01.
It was exactly 12 o'clock on the pip.   Wouldn't it be marvellous if only they could
run British Rail the same way as they run the RAF?

The specially equipped VC-10 flown by John to repatriate wounded troops.

John's flying ceased when, at forty-nine years of age, he suffered a medical problem which kept him grounded.   However, he served a further five years in a supervisory capacity at HQ Strike Command, finally retiring, aged fifty-five, in July 1992.   He says that he had a marvellous life in the RAF but left with one great regret - he didn't make the milestone of 10,000 flying hours as a pilot.   When his illness struck he only had 9814 hours 45 minutes !

However that's not quite the end of his long life in the RAF.   Classified as an ROIII, (Retired Officer III) he was offered an appointment as an Operations Officer at Brize Norton where he remained until finally retiring in March 2000.   Later that year he moved to Exmouth with his wife Anne and is now an active committee member of the East Devon Branch of the ACA.

1939-45 STAR - NOT INCLUDED !

George R.A. WOOTTON

Born in the East End of London in 1925, George Wootton left school in 1941 and, aged 16, started a career with the Westminster Bank. Then, on reaching his seventeenth birthday, he volunteered for aircrew duties in the RAF and after a wait was told to report to RAF Cardington for examinations and fitness tests. On their successful completion he was told he was suitable for training as a pilot, navigator or bomb aimer. He says, *"I was delighted. After all the air raids we'd suffered in my part of the world I would have the chance to get even."*

George subsequently became a member of the RAFVR on the 18th February 1943 and still has the letter telling him he was now an airman and must wait for his call-up papers. However these did not come until May 1944 when he was ordered to report to the ACRC at St. John's Wood, London, where he was told there was a surplus of pilots but he could become an air gunner. After initial 'square bashing' he was posted to the Air Gunnery School, Bridgnorth, where his flight was asked for a dozen men to train overseas.

His was one of the volunteers' names drawn from the hat but their destination still remained a mystery. The illustrative photograph was taken whilst George was on embarkation leave.

Ultimately George joined the converted troopship, the 'Reina del Pacifico', and with eight hundred other servicemen set sail from Greenock on the Clyde. Sailing northwards, they rounded the west coast of Ireland still unaware of their destination until a few days later they sailed past Gibraltar and entered the Mediterranean to head for Port Said. His ultimate destination was No.13 Air Gunners ITS at El Ballah, a desert airstrip a couple of miles from the Suez Canal.

After learning the intricacies of stripping and re-assembling the Browning machine gun whilst blindfold, the time came for actual flying. This was undertaken in the Anson when pupils would fire at target drogues towed behind Lysanders. These flights were usually of short duration and George's log showed he flew for 13.55 hours during which time he fired 3,300 rounds. He passed out on the 25th November 1944 with the second highest marks on his course.

Now a Sergeant, George's next move was to Palestine to join No.76 OTU at Aqir where they would fly the Wellington and gel as a new crew for the first time. Both he and his long-time friend, Dick Tindell, joined the crew of Rupert (Bob) Simpson. The Wellingtons had been well used, George reporting that in the first three days of 1945 they had to return three times from exercises, twice with engine failure and once with a u/s radio. Later that month three of the gunners sharing their billet were killed in a crash. The wheels of their aircraft were later washed up at Tel Aviv.

With OTU completion came a return to Egypt or, more precisely, to No.1675 HCU at Abu Suier where they arrived on the 14th February to convert onto the B24 Liberator.

202

Their own aircraft had once belonged to the Free Polish Air Force and according to George had *'seen better days'*. Furthermore he found his British made rear turret's movement by joy-stick rather imprecise and he looked forward to joining an operational Liberator squadron with their US built Consolidated Turret. It was here that, once again, tragedy seemed to follow George and his pal Dick. They shared their three-man billet with another gunner, a delightful character called Bill Impey. He was killed in a crash on the 23rd February and the arrival of the RAF Police to remove all his belongings had a profound effect on them.

Posting to an operational squadron followed successful completion of HCU and, for George and his pal Dick, this was to join No.40 Squadron based at Foggia Main in Italy. Its long history included tangling with the 'Red Baron' during WWI. However in WWII it was a bomber squadron and the Wellington bombers it had operated from Malta had been recently replaced by the Liberator. Their accommodation on arrival was abysmal, tents had been shredded by storms and many had been strengthened by use of packing cases. There were no beds or sheets and after a couple of nights sleeping on ground sheets, George found a part of a Liberator bomb bay which at least kept him off the ground. There were no baths, although some improvised showers had been made out of fighter drop tanks, and the food was awful. To cap it all George says, " *the local wine was poor and the little black dots in the bottles turned out to be small flies, You drank them if you wanted an alcoholic night. Larger blowflies hovered over the toilet, a plank with a hole over a large pit!* "

George flew his first 'op' on the 3rd April 1945 as a waist gunner on a raid against the Novska Marshalling Yards in Yugoslavia. Their aim was to delay German troop movements on the railway line between Belgrade and Zagreb. Carrying a 9,000 lbs bomb load, most of their ordnance hit the target despite the flak they encountered. His second 'op' was to come two days later, this time the target was the Monfalcone

Dockyards near Trieste in Northern Italy. At briefing they learned that it was the Adriatic base for German submarines and E-boats.   Unusually for RAF heavy bombers this was to be a daylight raid and they were to be escorted by USAAF Mustangs flown by the Tuskegee trained black airmen who boasted they had never lost a bomber. Indeed their boast held good.   All bombers returned and although one was hit by falling bombs from a higher aircraft it made base without any injuries.

George flew another eight 'ops' in the closing stages of the war.   These included attacks on the Austrian transport infrastructure at Innsbruck, from where his aircraft returned on three engines,   Villach and Freilassing.   They also attacked troop concentrations in Northern Italy.   His last flight was on the 7th May 1945, officially the 'last day' of the war in Europe.

Post war George returned to a banking career, rising to become manager of the Staines branch.   A 1948 honeymoon in Salcombe with his wife, Peggy, led to a love of the county and on retirement they set up home in Torquay.

Credited with a 'Good Tour', by a quirk of regulations George later learned he was not entitled to the award of the 1939-45 Star for they state: ' *The Star is awarded to all aircrew who took part in active operations against the enemy, subject to completion of two months in an operational unit and at least one operational sortie during the period from 3rd September 1939 to 8th May 1945"* .

Ironically for George,   whilst he had flown ten hazardous missions against heavily defended enemy targets, these had all been completed inside the two-month qualifying period.

"It makes one wonder at he ineptitude of those who make the Regulations",   was George's final comment.

THEIR LANCASTER WAS A 'WRITE-OFF'

Martin Clifford ('Cliff') WRIGHT, DFM

Cliff Wright was born in Plymouth on 1st June 1922 and educated in the city. On leaving school he became an insurance clerk but whilst still only eighteen years of age enlisted in the RAF and volunteered for aircrew. After ITW in the UK he was sent to Canada to undertake training as an observer at the RCAF Air Observer School, Portage La Prairie, where flying was undertaken in Ansons. There was further flying on the same type on his return to the UK when training continued at the RAF's Advanced Flying Unit at Wigtown in Scotland. It was now 1943 and Cliff's final preparation for operational flying came when he was posted to No.29 OTU at North Luffenham to fly on Wellingtons and then to No.1660 HCU at Swinderby to crew a Lancaster. Finally came the day for squadron service and Cliff and his crew were posted to join Bomber Command's No.9 (IX) Squadron at Bardney in Lincolnshire which operated Lancasters.

Cliff and his crew soon settled down to squadron life and had completed eleven ops over such targets as Hamburg, Munich, Mannheim, Hannover and the Ruhr. All, he describes as being without any real trouble from the enemy and with their worst moment coming when, through exceptionally bad weather on the Hannover raid, they lost most of the pilot's instruments, including air speed indicator, artificial horizon and altimeter and all their navigation aids. Fortunately by dead-reckoning and the pilot's skill they not only reached and successfully bombed their target, a fact confirmed by photographs, but also made it home. Their pilot was awarded an immediate DFC for a splendid piece of flying. However, for a graphic insight into the dangers all crews regularly faced here is Cliff's account of the operation they flew on the night of 3rd October 1943.

"Our squadron was putting on twelve aircraft in the first wave and we sat around our table in the briefing room looking anxiously at the black screen which covered the wall map that held the answer to all our thoughts - the target! Amongst our crew was a Sergeant Leslie who was standing in for our own mid-upper gunner who had a poisoned thumb and was grounded. The Squadron Commander pulled back the screen to reveal the target - KASSEL. Our route in would take us north of the Ruhr and out would be south of the Ruhr. There was nothing unusual at the briefing about the target and in common with most large German cities we were told to expect a strong concentration of anti-aircraft fire and searchlights.

At 1845 hours a signal from the control tower told us we could take off and we made a steady climb to operational height . It was a particularly dark night so we saw little of the rest of the bomber stream and no enemy activity. Within a few minutes of 'time on target' the pilot reported he could see no Pathfinder activity such as he would have expected or anything else for that matter. As navigator I then engaged in a rapid checking and reckoning of the navigation chart and my calculations, and confirmed we should be approaching the target. The pilot could still see nothing ahead and decided to orbit port. Then, just as he got part way into his turn both gunners shouted that the markers were going down ahead and to starboard. We were now lit up like a Christmas tree.

Almost at once both gunners sighted a Focke Wulf 190 at about 700 yards passing from starboard to port quarter and the rear gunner told the pilot to stand-by to corkscrew. As the enemy aircraft approached from the port quarter it turned to come in from dead astern. The rear gunner instructed the pilot to commence to corkscrew when the enemy aircraft was about 600 yards away and both gunners opened fire. At the same time the FW 190 opened fire with cannon and machine guns. His initial burst shot the cupola of the mid-upper turret away also cutting off

206

the electric and oxygen supplies to both turrets. Sgt. Leslie, the mid-upper gunner, was killed by a cannon shell through the head. The fighter continued to close in and at 300 yards both the fighter and Wally, our rear gunner, exchanged fire again. This time our gunner could see his shots entering the fighter's engine and it turned sharply to port, rolled over on its back and when alongside our Lancaster at about 100 yards it exploded. Pieces of fighter were blown against the Lancaster and Wally lost consciousness through lack of oxygen.

We were still over the now well illuminated target area at 20,000 feet and as soon as we had released our bombs our pilot, knowing both our gunners were out of action, put our nose down to leave as soon as possible. He lost height until oxygen was no longer needed which proved a wise decision because our rear gunner recovered and only suffered minor frostbite due to the loss of electricity to heat his flying suit.   We then set course for Ford, the nearest point in England where we could land and, flying at low level and away from the protection of the main bomber stream, we felt quite lonely.

After being airborne for some nine hours, we landed at Ford at 0400 hours but our personal relief and joy was saddened when the body of Sgt. Leslie was removed from the shattered turret. A stranger to us, he had died because our own gunner had a poisoned thumb. Fate pays some strange hands. Our aircraft was a sorry sight. The mid-upper turret was missing, the fuselage was peppered from middle to tail from cannon and machine gun fire and pitted with fragments from the enemy fighter's explosion which also twisted the tailplane.   It was subsequently pronounced a 'write-off'.

We were now safely in England but penniless as it was not permitted to take money on operations. Fortunately a kind civilian engineer from Avro learned of our plight and took us all into Littlehampton for a pint ! However we still faced the problem of getting back to Bardney in Lincolnshire. We had no flyable aircraft, were grimy, unshaven, dressed in full flying kit and carrying our harnesses and parachutes. All the RAF did was to give us a railway warrant for a journey which included a tube ride across London. What a sight we were ! When we arrived back to base we learned that Wally had been credited with shooting down the FW 190, they couldn't very well argue because we brought back the bits to prove it ! He was awarded the DFM and we all went into Boston to celebrate."

A question of logistics meant a switch to another Lancaster squadron, No.44, based at Dunholme Lodge, Lincolnshire. Cliff went on to complete his tour with them and was awarded the DFM on 6th June 1944. A short period instructing at No.1654 HCU Wigsley ensued, during which he was commissioned, followed by a posting to No.142 Squadron at Gransden Lodge to fly the much faster and versatile Mosquito. He was to complete another twenty-two ops with them, attacking an assortment of enemy targets, often at low level. When hostilities ended he spent a brief spell with No.608 Squadron before being switched to Transport Command's No.162 Squadron at Blackbushe which operated Mosquitoes on urgent despatch and diplomatic post runs to destinations throughout Europe and the Middle East.

Cliff had survived fifty-two raids over occupied Europe and was released from service in August 1946. Shortly afterwards he joined the former Plymouth City Police, now part of the Devon and Cornwall Constabulary. He served all his time within the city, retiring as a Chief Inspector in 1972 to take up a civilian appointment within the Force.

He finally retired, aged 65, in June 1987 and continues to live in the city with his wife, Betty.

Top: Cliff Wright having a 'cuppa' as a Sergeant Navigator on Lancasters.
Below: Cliff, on the right and now commissioned, stands beneath one of
the engines of his Mosquito with his pilot.

RAF or NAVY ? NO PROBLEM - HE FLEW FOR BOTH !

Frank YOUNG

Frank was born in London in October 1923 and, after leaving the Henry Thornton School, briefly followed a career in accountancy. However, having volunteered for aircrew, he enlisted in the RAF on the 9th November 1942, shortly after his nineteenth birthday. After his initial ground training at No.7 ITW Newquay, he was selected to complete his flying training in Canada and in August 1943 had the great experience of making the Atlantic crossing on the Queen Mary. Even more interesting was the fact that amongst the passengers were Winston Churchill, his wife and daughter Mary, plus senior military commanders, which included Lord Portal, and Wg.Cdr. Guy Gibson VC. Apparently they were on a mission to persuade President Roosevelt that the offensive in Europe was more important than the Far East. Voyage completed, Frank duly arrived at No.31 EFTS at RCAF De Winton in Alberta where his primary trainer was the Fairchild Cornell, a two-seat open-cockpit low-wing monoplane with a fixed undercarriage. Completion of Phase One saw him moving to another RCAF base in Alberta, this time to No.34 SFTS at Medicine Hat. Here advanced flying was on the North American Harvard. Receiving his RAF pilot's wings at the end of the course,

Frank was commissioned and returned to the UK and a period of frustration.

Anxious to see action, he seemed to be either on leave or attending seemingly non-essential courses. However he did use the lull to get married ! In August 1944 Frank was presented with a golden opportunity when the Royal Navy became short of pilots. He immediately volunteered and officially left the RAF on the 29th October 1944 to become Sub Lieutenant (A) Frank Young RNVR the following day!

An almost immediate change in flying ensued when he was posted to undergo conversion on the naval version of the Spitfire, the Seafire, with No.761 Squadron at RNAS Henstridge This was followed by a posting to the Far East in June 1945 and a month later to N.O.T.U. at Tambaram, Madras, India where he completed a specialist course in ground attack and dive-bombing, still flying the Seafire Mk.IIIB.

The photograph above is of Frank making his first deck landing with a Seafire, hooking and tripping the wire on the short deck escort carrier, HMS Ravager.
The header is of Frank whilst serving with 894 Squadron aboard HMS Indefatigable.

However, by now the war in Europe had come to an end, while that against the Japanese was rapidly drawing to a close and Frank's expectations of being involved in the final offensive never materialised with the dropping of the Atomic bomb. However, he was flown to the Pacific area and joined 894 Squadron on *HMS INDEFATIGABLE* as a replacement for pilots lost with 24 Wing. He served aboard her until flying off the Carrier on March 15th 1946 to land at Gosport, Hampshire.

Four months later, on the 5th July 1946, his Royal Navy Service came to an end. However this was not the end of his flying, for the following year he switched back to the RAF again when he joined the RAFVR. He was to fly with them for six years, until 1953, during which time he became a QFI (Qualified Flying Instructor).

When his flying ended he entered another phase of reserve service with a switch to intelligence duties, a role he performed until 1966. As a result of his long service in the reserve forces he received the Air Efficiency Award and, later, a clasp.

Subsequent to leaving full time military service, Frank began a distinguished career in Education, obtaining both a BA and as B.Sc (Econ) from London University. He later returned to the Far East where he became Headmaster of RAF Grammar School, Changi, which provided education for the children of servicemen serving in Singapore and Malaysia. With the withdrawal of British Forces from the area, and the ultimate closure of the Changi base, he returned to the UK to resume his education career as Headmaster of Bridgnorth Grammar School which he guided through a process of change and development to a 11-18 Comprehensive School of more than a thousand places.

Today he lives in Sidmouth with Donelda, his wife.

OTHER AIRCRAFT MENTIONED IN THE BOOK

Readers will have noticed that some aircraft, such as the Lancaster and Halifax, have been frequently mentioned in the book and that at least one photograph illustrating that aircraft will have been printed somewhere within its pages.   However, a number of other types have been mentioned but space precluded their inclusion within the narrative.   Some of these aircraft are illustrated in the following pages.

Two fighter aircraft seen flying from most Devon airfields during WWII were
the Spitfire (top) and the Hurricane (above).

The Ventura, seen above, occasionally operated from RAF Exeter.

The USAAF B-17 Flying Fortress

It occasionally used RAF Dunkeswell where this one was photographed.

The Boulton Paul Defiant was operated from both RAF Exeter and RAF Roborough.

The Fairey Battle operated by No.2 AACU at RAF Roborough.

The USAAF P-38 Lightning - a surprise visitor to RNAS Haldon in 1941.

Top (left): The Bristol Blenheim. Norman Conquer was the sole survivor when one of these crashed at RAF Bicester on the 11th November 1941. (see page 93).

Top (right): The Messerschmitt Bf 109. A pair of these attacked RAF Bolt Head on the 7th March 1942, damaging a Spitfire of No. 317 Squadron as it was taking off. (see page 35).

Bottom: The Avro Manchester. Similar in appearance to the Lancaster but with only two engines. It also proved unreliable. It was used by 1661 HCU at RAF Winthorpe in 1943 and flown by Ken Cook. (see page 98).

In the early post war period the RAF's main fighter squadrons comprised the Vampire and the Meteor, the latter coming in a number of variants.

The RAF's only jet fighter to see action in WWII was the Meteor Mks I & III. In the early post war period the Mks 4 & 8 formed the backbone of the RAF's day fighter squadrons. Shown above in a Meteor 4 which was flown by David Blair, Vic Dabin and 'Griff' Griffith amongst others.

Shown above is a Vampire FB 9. Designed as a fighter-bomber, the Vampire first flew in 1943 but did not enter squadron service until April 1946. The aircraft depicted here was flown by the author in 1953.

GLOSSARY

ACRC.   - Air Crew Reception Centre.
AFS.   - Advanced Flying School.
AONS.   - Air Observer Navigation School.
B&GS.   - Bombing & Gunnery School.
EFTS.   - Elementary Flying Training School.
FCU.   - Fighter Control Unit.
FTS.   - Flying Training School.
HCU.   - Heavy Conversion Unit.
HMAFV.   - Her Majesty's Air Force Vessel.
ITS.   - Initial Training School (post-war).
ITW.   - Initial Training Wing. (war-time).
OCU.   - Operational Conversion Unit (post-war).
OTU.   - Operational Training Unit . (war-time).
R.Aux.A.F..   - Royal Auxiliary Air Force.
RAFVR.   - Royal Air Force Volunteer Reserve.
SFTS.   - Service Flying Training School.
W.Op/AG.   - Wireless Operator/Air Gunner.

Plt.Off.   - Pilot Officer.
Flg.Off.   - Flying Officer.
Flt.Lt.   - Flight Lieutenant.
Sqn.Ldr.   - Squadron Leader.
Wg.Cdr.   - Wing Commander.
Gp.Cpt.   - Group Captain.
Air Cdre.   - Air Commodore.
AVM.   - Air Vice Marshal.
AM.   - Air Marshal.
ACM.   - Air Chief Marshal.
Marshal of the Royal Air Force.

The East Devon Branch
of The AirCrew Association

wishes to thank those whose generosity has made the publication of this book possible. Some like the Palace Hotel have histories inextricably linked to the Royal Air Force and many aircrew recruits will remember the Templestowe, Sefton and other Torbay hotels. Others have become favourite haunts for many of our monthly pub lunches and social events. We thank all those who have helped us and hope that you, as readers, will support them in return.

The Palace Hotel
Torquay
* * * *

We are proud to have played an important role in the lives of so many wounded aircrew and congratulate The AirCrew Association on the production of this book. Our archives record the events described within these pages but today we look forward to inviting guests to enjoy our luxurious surroundings, excellent cuisine and perhaps a round of golf on our championship course.

For further details please telephone 01803 -200200
or visit our website at www.palacetorquay.co.uk

The publication of this book has been partly funded by a grant from

'Awards for All'

'Awards for All' is a joint Lottery grants programme supported by

The Arts Council England

Big Lottery Fund *

Heritage Lottery Fund

Sport England

* Big Lottery Fund is the joint operating name of the New Opportunities Fund

and the National Lottery Charities Board

(which makes grants under the name of the Community Fund)

The important role played by many hotels in Devon during WWII has featured in the earlier pages of this book.   For many young aircrew recruits this was their first introduction to service life.   Many were later killed, Bomber Command alone losing over 55,000 men. Other survived to tell their stories.

The following hotels were amongst those who played a part in those young lives and have been mentioned, albeit sometimes briefly, within the pages of this book.   Today they have expressed a wish to be involved with its publication.

The Sefton Hotel,   Babbacombe Downs Road, Torquay.

The Templestowe Hotel, Tor Church Road, Torquay.

The Bedford Hotel, The Esplanade, Sidmouth.

To be part of history why not visit them whilst in the area. Then, as you enjoy their 21st century amenities, try to imagine what life was like there over sixty years ago !

INTERNATIONAL AIRPORT

Exeter International Airport is proud to commemorate the history of the airfield serving as a wartime aerodrome during the 2nd World War, and is pleased to sponsor the East Devon Branch of the AirCrew Association in publishing this book.

Situated in the Heart of the West Country, at the focus of an excellent communications network, Exeter International Airport serves the residents and businesses in Devon, Cornwall, Somerset and Dorset.   It offers an excellent choice of holiday destinations for the West Country traveller together with direct scheduled services with FlyBe to destinations in the UK, Eire and Western Europe.   For further information telephone 01392 367433.

Flying you further .... from closer to home !

The Cat & Fiddle.
A 16th century inn on the A3052,
Exeter to Sidmouth Road, at Clyst
St. Mary near the Westpoint
Showground.
We are pleased to welcome
the East Devon Branch of the
AirCrew Association on the
occasion of their 'pub lunches'
and happy to assist in the
sponsorship of their book.

'Where good comradeship enjoys good food !'

The following hotels and inns, which are also used by members of the East Devon Branch of The AirCrew Association for the holding of their many social events, have also expressed a wish to be involved with the sponsorship of this book.

The Devoncourt Hotel, Douglas Avenue, Exmouth.
The Manor Hotel, The Beacon, Exmouth.
The Mount Pleasant Inn, Dawlish Warren.

We enjoy their hospitality and hope you will too !

We'll Meet Again

Fantastic Fun-Filled Holidays With A 40's Theme
*Hotel Decorated in 40's Theme *Staff In Uniform
*Soldiers *Sailors *Airman *ARP's *Wrens *Waafs *
*Sandbags *Camouflage *Flags *Wartime Memorabilia

At The Majestic Templestowe Hotel
TORQUAY

Departures From Friday 3rd March until Wednesday 26th April

•SOUNDS OF THE 40's•
**Top Torquay Duo Present
"Sounds Of Miller" "Andrews Sisters"
& Much More**

•ROLL OUT THE BARREL•
**V.E. Celebration Party Night
Fancy Dress - 40's Theme**

4 Days 3 Nights From £119 To £139

Sea-view Supplement £9 per person

Holidays Include:-
*All Coach Travel
*3 Nights Dinner Bed & Breakfast
*All Rooms En-Suite
*Great Excursions
*Fantastic Hotel Atmosphere
*Brilliant Entertainment
*Hotel Fully Decorated in 40's Decor
*Staff In Uniform

Excursions Include:-
•**HALF DAY**: To Teignmouth:- The wartime port where many of the motor torpedo boats were constructed. Frequently bombed during the war due to it's strategic significance
•**FULL DAY**: To Dartmouth & Slapton:- Visit to this historic naval town where part of the invasion fleet assembled. Then onto Slapton Sands, Site of the D-Day Landing Rehearsals

To Book Telephone 01626 770246

NOTES